Homosexuality AND THE AUTHORITY OF Scripture

J. Elliott Lein

*A personal exploration of the
Biblical perspective on homosexuality
with a focus on six passages:*

GENESIS 19:4-5
LEVITICUS 18:22
LEVITICUS 20:13

1 TIMOTHY 1:9-10
1 CORINTHIANS 6:9
ROMANS 1:26-27

HOMOSEXUALITY AND THE AUTHORITY OF SCRIPTURE
How a Fundamentalist-Raised, Bible Church-Attending, Evangelical Christian Missionary Came to Reconcile the Authority of Scripture and Affirmation of Same-Sex Marriage

Copyright © 2016 J. Elliott Lein

www.jelliottlein.com

Creative Commons License: Attribution-ShareAlike 4.0 International
You are free to share (copy and redistribute the material in any medium or format) and adapt (remix, transform, and build upon the material) under the following terms:

> *Attribution — You must give appropriate credit, provide a link to the license, and indicate if changes were made. You may do so in any reasonable manner, but not in any way that suggests the licensor endorses you or your use.*
>
> *ShareAlike — If you remix, transform, or build upon the material, you must distribute your contributions under the same license as the original.*

Published in the United States by J. Elliott Lein.

PAPERBACK ISBN 978-1-5146-1426-6

Read it free online at gaymarriageandthebible.com

Printed on demand in the United States of America
CreateSpace Independent Publishing Platform
2016 – First Edition

Unless otherwise indicated, all Scripture quotations are from New Revised Standard Version Bible, copyright 1989, Division of Christian Education of the National Council of the Churches of Christ in the United States of America. Used by permission. All rights reserved.

Arno Pro (body: 11.5/16)
Proxima Nova Extra Condensed

*For my beloved family and friends
in Siloam Springs, Arkansas.*

Contents

PART I

Introduction: *My Journey and Our Questions* 1

A Case for the Possibility of Changing our Minds 16

PART II

The Tale of Sodom and Gomorrah in Genesis 19:4-5 48

An Abomination in Leviticus 18:22 75

The Death Penalty in Leviticus 20 88

What are the Arsenokoites in 1 Timothy 1:9? 104

The Effeminate & Sodomites in 1 Corinthians 6:19 130

Unnatural Acts in Romans 1:26-27 161

PART III

The Spirit Speaking Through Experience 191

Concluding Thoughts 205

Appendix: Marriage in the Bible 210

*Can you hold to the authority of Scripture
and support same-sex marriage at the same time?*

~ CHAPTER 1 ~
Introduction

Christian community in the United States is bitterly divided over sexual orientation and same-sex marriage today. The debate is splitting denominations, churches, and families. Many people who grew up in the church are leaving, either forced out by rejection or voluntarily in solidarity with those they believe are being wronged.

For many Christians the debate is deeper than the surface question of sexual ethics or political policy. Our understanding of the authority of the Bible (especially for Protestants) and Christian Tradition (especially for Catholics and the Orthodox) is at stake, and the affirming perspective on being gay and same-sex marriage appears to threaten the foundations of our faith.

This is legimately scary and worrying. I do not wish to minimize these concerns. Yet we must seriously engage with the questions of our time. We cannot ignore or dismiss them, in either a conservative or progressive direction. I believe that the Bible is vital to our faith and relevant in our time, and that it speaks anew to every age through the guidances of the Spirit.

This is about an orthodox Christian response to homosexuality and same-sex marriage

I am writing for a generally conservative evangelical Christian audience, beginning with my friends and family, who want to know why some Christians like myself are taking affirming positions on gay marriage and homosexuality while simultaneously holding a high view of Scripture. It is the work of one straight, married man who has been studying and thinking on these questions for the past few years.

Setting the stage

It's important to be sure we share an understanding of the basics before diving into the content of this book.

Three Christian community responses to homosexuality

Here are the three main responses that Christians have to the question of same-sex orientation:

Sinful Choice Response: Homosexuality is a deliberate lifestyle choice and a sin. It is the epitome of rebellion against God and a sign of pursuing worldly lusts instead of Christ. For some of the most concerned parties, all sexual activity between same-gender partners is a crime against society and should be punished through the judicial system.

Temptation Response: Homosexual desire is a symptom of the fall, and is a temptation to sin no different than the pattern of heterosexual adultery or greed. Those who struggle with same-sex attraction (SSA) are no more sinners than the rest of us in the desire alone. Christians must encourage and support our brothers and sisters in lifelong celibacy with no hope of marriage (this is known in some circles as 'Side B'), or in pursuing a marriage with the opposite sex in spite of their orientation. This view holds that sexual activity between same-gender partners in any context is a sin.

Affirming Response: Being gay or bisexual is part of how some of us are created by God, and we can encourage all our siblings in Christ to find good and holy expression of their God-created orientation through consensual, lifelong, monogamous marriage (this is sometimes called 'Side A').

In the American evangelical Christian community, most held to the *Sinful Choice Response* through the 1990s. Now many, through seeing testimonies and research, have moved to the *Temptation Response* above. In the last few years, a small but growing percentage of those who claim the title "Evangelical Christians" are moving to the *Affirming Response*. They are following some of their brothers and sisters in Christ from some mainline denominations who have accepted gay folks as equals in life and marriage for some decades now.

The big questions on the Bible and homosexuality

This leads to serious questions amongst both accepting and non-accepting groups.

1. Are all Christians who choose the *Affirming Response* either abandoning their faith and Scripture, or encouraging their fellow believers to remain in sinful lifestyles

for which they will face temporal and/or eternal negative consequences?
2. Can an individual affirm the continued authority of Scripture for Christian living and support same-sex marriage at the same time?

These are very important questions for the global Christian church today. I'm assuming that the reader recognizes that being gay or bisexual is not a choice, and that there are faithful God-honoring Christians who are attracted to the same gender without conscious choice, whether they are in relationships or celibate. If this is a new idea for you, please consider listening to some testimonies, some of which I have collected on this book's website at *Gaymarriageandthebible.com/further-research*

What I believe

"I desire the covenant and sacrament
of life-long monagamous marriage
as the ideal context for sexual expression,
the uniting of two souls in one relationship,
and ultimately the reflection of God's love,
to be available for all people as
consensual adults, gay or straight."
   — *My current statement on the topic*

Given my background, many of my conservative friends and family assume that I can only give the statement above if I have rejected the authority of the Bible for our lives. I have written this book to show why I disagree. I believe that there is an option, and in fact a calling from the Spirit and shown in Scripture, to embrace both the Bible and the love between same-sex couples.

What about the middle ground?

There are many conservative Christians who embrace their fellow gay Christ-followers in love, as made in God's image, yet cannot condone marriage for same-sex couples. I understand their motivations and heart for people, and I agreed with them for a long time, but I cannot do so any longer. The three main recommendations from this perspective are:

Reparative ("Ex-gay") Therapy: Some of the largest organizations[1] that were a part of this work for decades have shut down in acknowledgement that an actual change in experienced orientation does not happen for nearly all people who seek it, and is not healthy for most people.[2] The best programs can at the most help a small percentage to live with their same-sex desires without seeking a same-sex partner (which leads to the next two options). Russell Moore, leader of the Southern Baptists' Ethics and Religious Liberty Commission and proponent of the Temptation Response, publicly denounced reparative therapy as "severely counterproductive".[3] The American Association of Christian Counselors now recommends that its 50,000 members

---

1 e.g. Exodus International, led by Alan Chambers and John Paulk

2 Sam Brinton testifies to experiencing shock therapy combined with gay porn, and being convinced that he's the last gay person left because the government killed all the rest and that all gay men have AIDS. http://bit.ly/HS-brinton

3 "Evangelical leader Russell Moore denounces ex-gay therapy" by Sarah Pulliam Bailey in Religion News Service, October 28, 2014

counsel for celibacy, not reparative therapy.

Traditional Marriage: As part of the ex-gay philosophy, many gay individuals have been encouraged to marry the opposite sex and remain committed regardless of any same-sex attraction they have. This appears to work out fine for some, but I have heard many stories and know people personally where this works out tragically for both partners and children in the long run. This cannot be the only answer for all gay Christians.

Lifelong Celibacy: Our apostle Paul was a strong advocate of celibacy in his epistles, and we know of many saints whose celibacy has given them space for great ministry. Some openly gay Christians are joyfully choosing this option.[4] However, there is a significant difference in forced celibacy due to birth rather than of chosen celibacy out of a calling. This is larger than simply sexual drive (a large part of who we are as humans to start with)—it is blocking any access to the life-sharing committed relationships that are freely offered to heterosexual Christian couples (regardless of their maturity or wisdom). Having this as the only option has led many gay Christians to exist in despair and depression, sometimes leading to self-harm or suicide, or abandon the faith.

When you hear testimonies of people who pray daily, sometimes for decades, for a change of their same-sex orientation, and never experience a difference, it's hard to think that this is something God plans to change for most people. Facing a lifetime without the hope of ever having an intimate life partner

---

4 See *Washed and Waiting* by Wesley Hill, for example

INTRODUCTION

is also daunting and troubling.

Even though I am not gay, I saw the dilemma my fellow Christians were facing, and knew I had to join them in this search of the Bible. Following is a brief version of how this happened:

My journey

I'll answer the following questions to help you understand a little bit more about how I came to write this book.

- Why would I research and write something like this?
- What perspective is it coming from?

I was raised in a good conservative fundamentalist and evangelical Christian home and church. There are many things to say, and value, about that. What is relevant for this topic is that I grew up assuming the following things:

- that the Protestant Christian Bible we read in English (generally using the NIV translation) is our complete and self-sufficient rulebook for Christian faith and all of life,
- that it provides us all the answers we need with consistent and unchanging interpretation,
- and that it clearly and unambiguously tells us all sex and desire outside of a heterosexual marriage is wrong.

All that being said, I have a confession to make. For decades I valued the Bible in principle, but rarely read it for myself. Sure, I knew personal devotional reading was a general religious expectation, but I never experienced much valuein the practice for me personally. I had pastors and teachers explaining it to me all my life, and every time I opened it up I thought "I know what that's about from Sunday School" and lost interest.

It wasn't until I began attending a Bible study started by my Bible Church pastor a few years ago around age 30 that this began to very gradually change. In this group we started with Genesis 1, and began reading long passages (10-20 chapters per week). We would then be challenged to think about and discuss what we read – not what we remembered from past lessons. By the time we reached the New Testament two years later, I had started realizing that there was so much more depth and excitement in the text than I had ever thought possible, and my love for Scripture was born.

A brief conversation with a friend

Several years ago my wife and I decided to quit my career, sell everything, and become missionaries overseas. We spent a year raising support by meeting individually with people all over the country and asking for financial and prayer assistance.

On the verge of getting on the plane in January of 2012, I had a pivotal conversation over email with a business colleague and friend. I had been working with him on various projects over the last few years and always enjoyed our relationship, though we have never met in person. He had been following our journey online, and he reached out to ask:

> "As you may know, I am a gay dude, made by God. I will happily support your work if I know you don't discriminate against me. Let me know."

I knew my friend was gay, and had been with his partner in California for longer than I had been married, so I wasn't surprised to hear this. I reached out to him with the message I understood at the time: affirming his faith (with the traditional "we're all sinners" language) and inherent value as created by God, but saying that I could not affirm his sexuality because the Bible was very clear on this.

He was gracious and kind in our series of responses, but it was clear we would continue to disagree on this point. Initially I was proud of my half of the conversation. I felt that I had demonstrated an open and kind attitude to the topic, but that I had stood firmly for the truth.

Over the following year I could not shake this conversation. I thought about it every few weeks, and there was one thing that I began to be uncomfortable with. No matter how I rephrased the message, or thought about the implications, there was nothing I could say from the traditional position that would completely affirm my friend as a good creation of God without requiring him to change who he deeply knew himself to be as a fellow believer in Christ. My pride in how graciously and lovingly I handled this began to change into realizing that there was very little practical difference in the end for my friend between my message and the condemnation language of Westboro Baptist Church.

I wasn't sure what to do with this idea. I couldn't throw out the Bible just to "make my friend feel good," yet I also was troubled with the feeling that what I felt forced to say was unloving in some fundamental way.

What is sin anyway?

Another part of my journey came out of my continued reading and study of the Bible. As I read continuously through the Scriptures, I began seeing a pattern in what was called out as sin by God. Up until this point I assumed that sin was a fairly arbitrary thing from a human perspective—if God said that something was off-limits or separated us from him, then that was that.

What I began to see is the deep connection between lists of sins and behaviors that harm and break community and relationships between people. Stealing, lying, adultery, and gossip all have a direct negative effect on those around us. The one sin that didn't always seem to fit this mold was same-sex attraction within a covenant relationship. I could see that not all gay couples were promiscuous or seeming to be engaging in empirically harmful behavior, just as not all straight couples avoided these things.

I started wondering why this didn't always seem to fit the pattern, and decided to start doing some more reading.

Searching

I began to read more stories online of believers, growing up in conservative Christian homes and deeply devoted to God, who reached adolescence and found to their horror that they were attracted exclusively to the same sex. I read of how depressed and suicidal they became, knowing that their unasked-for feelings and every expression of love through a physical relationship that they could imagine were seen as corrupt and rejected completely by the God they loved.

After many months of reading and thinking, I realized that I was no longer as certain of the interpretation of the Bible that I had always heard on this topic. By the summer of 2014 I had decided I would no longer be able to tell my friend that he was wrong. Several months later, after more conversations and research, I finally changed my mind completely. I am personally convinced that the truest expression of our faith, founded on the Bible, is seen in offering our brothers and sisters the opportunity to join together in consensual, monogamous, committed marriage regardless of gender.

Why I wrote this book

While I had read a number of books on this topic, and hundreds of articles online, I had not done my own study of the Scriptures before making my decision.

Around the time that this happened, our family returned from the mission field and I entered the discernment process for ordination in the Episcopal church. When we told my family about our plans, one family member reached out in concern over this particular issue.

During the course of our email dialog in the fall of 2014, I was asked to respond to the following (among similar related questions):

- *How do you explain the following passages in the Bible: Leviticus 18:21-22 and 20:13, Romans 1:25-27, I Corinthians 6:9-11?*
- *Can the hermeneutic you use on those passages be applied to any other passages?*
- *How does that affect the gospel?*

Initially, I planned to write an email in response with a brief summary of the arguments I had read. I can't even recall now how exactly this whole project actually started, but I found myself doing my own research for the first time. That little email has grown into this book. I'm very grateful for the challenge to explore this topic on my own, and the love that was expressed for us in the concern from this beloved family member.

I will be focusing on the small set of verses that are generally understood to be specifically against all homosexuality. I've added two sections from Genesis (covering Jude as well) and 1 Timothy to the list above.

Wherever you are on this topic, or wherever you end up, I hope this book is helpful and illuminating for all those who are wondering why some Christians like myself do not think that affirming love and marriage for same-sex couples requires throwing out the authority of Scripture.

Reading the Bible

Before we begin, here's some background on my methods in research and writing.

How I did my research

First, please note that I am not nor do I claim to be a Bible scholar. I do not know Hebrew, Greek or Latin, and I have not read any untranslated original source material. **Everything I have read is accessible to the average reader.** I have read many books that have helped me generate some ideas and perspectives, but most of my resources are freely available online. The Bible itself will function as both primary source as well as the subject of the discussion.

I will not be citing work in an exhaustive academic way. I will assume some level of trust at certain points that I am doing my best to be accurate when referring to various things I bring up. This doesn't mean that every claim I reference is the one option available, but merely that I have tried to make sure there is some collective agreement that what I'm saying is a viable interpretation. If you have a question about a specific item, please do your own research to verify. You'll likely find the same material I have by simply doing an online search.

I do not claim to have found unshakable proof of anything. I am certain I can be, and am, wrong about many things. In fact, I'm eager for readers to send me corrections, additions or refutations. In the end, this is simply my own flawed attempt to figure out this very tough topic for my own use. I hope it can be useful for others as well, whether you agree or disagree with the conclusions by the end.

Because of my research methods, I hope that you will be able to follow along with your own research using the base I'm laying out, if that's something that interests you.

Research and source notes

I am using the New Revised Standard Version (NSRV) translation of the Bible for the primary quotes, since it is the version many Biblical scholars recommend. If you don't like this translation, please feel free to reference your own. There is no substantial difference in translation of the key words we'll be looking at. I have cross-referenced a number of other translations while writing such as the Young's Literal Translation (YLT) and both Greek and Hebrew interlinear translations. I'm using the conservative standard Strong's Exhaustive Concordance (in addition to some more up-to-date resources) to research the Hebrew and Greek words, and I have provided the Strong's reference numbers for each one that I bring up in the text. Most of these resources are freely available online so that all readers can follow along.

I used BibleHub.com for both the Strong's references as well as the interlinear readings. I prefer BibleGateway.com's website for comparing different translations which we'll be doing a lot.

I took the liberty of reclaiming the King James Version's translation word choice of "effeminate" for the title of the section on 1 Corinthians 6:9-10. This is also the word used in Young's Literal Translation. The reason will become clear as you read.

Notes on dates and terms

For dates I'm using the BCE/CE notation. The term "Christian / Common / Current Era" was first used in 1584 CE, and has been gaining acceptance since the 19th century at the urging of Jewish scholars. No rejection of the origin of the numbering (based on Christ's estimated birthdate by a monk in 525 CE – he was only off by a few years!) is implied by this.

I've chosen to use the Hebrew term *"Tanakh"* to refer to what Christians have traditionally called the Old Testament. It seems more specific and honoring of the Hebrew community to whom God first revealed himself in the Scriptures. If you're not familiar with the term, *Tanakh* is an acronym from the three sections of the Jewish Bible: *Torah* (Teachings or Law), *Nevi'im* (Prophets) and *Ketuvim* (Writings)—hence *Ta-Na-Kh*. As a side note, the "Prophets" include what we would consider the books of prophecy and Joshua, Judges, Samuel and Kings (but not Chronicles). When New Testament writers referred to "the Law and the Prophets" they were speaking of the two highest-regarded and first-canonized sections of the *Tanakh*. The Psalms, Proverbs and other books complete the Hebrew Bible in the

Writings section, and were accepted into the Scripture canon just a few hundred years before Jesus was born.

Starting our read

This book started as a simple email response in a personal conversation. It has grown a lot over the last year of revisions. I pray you find it helpful, wherever you end up on the final conclusions.

There have been many books written on this subject from a variety of perspectives. You will find a list of additional resources at the end of this book.

What you will find in this book

We will be focused primarily on the translation and interpretation of certain words and phrases found in six key passages in the Bible. The case I would like to make for you is that the current accepted translations and understandings of these verses are subjective and opinionated, and that there are other options we may consider without abandoning a traditional view of the authority of the Bible.

"Why would/should Christians ever consider rethinking this issue?"

CHAPTER 2
A Case for the Possibility of Changing our Minds

Before we open the Bible itself, it's important to provide a response to the question above. After all, the average conservative Christian today has been perfectly happy with our standard reading of the Bible against homosexuality and same-sex marriage for a long time. Why would we even ask these questions?

In this chapter, we will look at why it is so important to return to a sincere study of the Bible on the topic of homosexuality. We will explore the following two questions:

1. Are there any parallels in the Christian tradition for changing our minds on long-standing orthodox perspectives such as this?
2. Are there any compelling reasons to spend time working on this particular question?

I would like to answer these two questions by making a case that we can agree on each of the following four assertions:

1. The Bible has always been and continues to be interpreted in different ways.
2. History shows that Christians have often rethought previously orthodox interpretations of the Scriptures.
3. Much harm has and is coming to gay people in our community from the conservative position.
4. Our Christian community is fragmenting, and many are rejecting our faith tradition over this issue.

We'll start with looking at what it means to interpret the Bible, as distinct from simply reading it.

Is the Bible simply read, or is it interpreted?

The first question every Christian must ask is:

> *"Is it possible to change our minds*
> *about an interpretation of the Bible*
> *without rejecting its authority?"*

Unfortunately, my personal experience in the conservative evangelical Christian community did not give me the foundation to understand this question. I had a tragic lack of knowledge of church history and how things have changed over time. This may not hold true for all readers, of course.

I have gained much by beginning to correct this gap in my understanding of our faith, through personal reading and the encouragement of my new church community in the global and historic Anglican Communion. As I've found, there are deeply marvelous or profoundly disturbing variations in understandings over time, depending on your perspective. My personal conclusion has been that God must somehow be ok, even maybe actively encouraging, the variety of our beliefs.

Translation as interpretation

It has been important for my journey to realize that there is no one final and unchanging reading of the Bible. Some people refer to this concept when we use the word *interpretation*.

The most basic, straight-forward level of interpretation starts with the fact that the Christian Bible is a collection of 66 (or 73, or 77, depending on your church tradition) independently written texts that were originally set down in ancient Hebrew, Aramaic, and Koine Greek. Every Christian who reads the Bible in a language other than these three is reading a translation. Every translation is a form of interpretation, especially when coming from languages that are 2,000 to 3,000 years old and are no longer in common use (modern Hebrew and Greek are functionally different languages).

It is one thing to translate from Spanish to French, or German to English. Even as similar as these languages are, with common roots, translators have to make judgement calls on how to best communicate a concept in the target language.

When we go back to ancient and especially non-Western languages it gets much more complicated. Words in ancient Hebrew (containing approximately 8,000 words) can mean many different things in English (with about 660,000 words), either changing based on context, or conveying many meanings all at the same time. We understand the definition of most words, but some have been lost to the ages and we must guess at the original intent. The Greek text of the New Testament is closer to modern languages such as English, and easier to reference because of the volume of other literature written in it, but it is still not something we can simply plug words into a mechanical replacement device.

Every translation is an interpretation simply getting it into the target language. There is so much more that could be said about translating the Bible which we don't have space to cover here, but it is a fascinating topic.

The second level of interpretation during translation comes from the unavoidable bias of those who are translating. Even the most careful and impartial scholars must make subjective choices of words and meanings. This is part of why we have so many different translations (over 100 currently in print) to choose from today in English, from very strict literal translations like the YLT or NRSV to what are called "dynamic equivalents" like The Message. Most are somewhere in between, but none are exactly the same as the original texts.

Tanakh interpretation example: *Ishmael*

Here's an example of how difficult it can be to accurately translate ancient Hebrew in particular, and how that can have a dramatic effect on our lives and understanding.

In Genesis chapter 16, the angel of the Lord pronounces a blessing on the pregnant Hagar, the concubine of Abraham, after she had been driven from their home by the jealous Sarah. Here is the traditional rendering of the blessing:

"I will so greatly multiply your offspring
>that they cannot be counted for multitude...

Now you have conceived and shall bear a son;
> you shall call him Ishmael,
> for the Lord has given heed to your affliction.

He shall be a wild ass of a man,
with his hand against everyone,
> and everyone's hand against him;
and he shall live at odds with all his kin."
— Genesis 16:10-12

This translation that we normally see in our Bibles gives a decidedly mixed blessing that has contributed to tension and conflict in Jewish-Christian-Muslim relations, as Ishmael is the ancestor of the Arabic tribes who remain in conflict with the descendents of his brother Isaac, the Israelites.

Yet there are other ways to translate those same words. The reputable Judaica Press translation has verse 12 reading:

And he will be a wild donkey of a man,
his hand will be upon all,
> and everyone's hand upon him,
and before all his brothers he will dwell.

Some interpreters suggest one more layer, that the preposition translated as "against" or "upon" can be "with" instead. Others say that the phrase "wild ass" is more accurately "fruitful man" which fits with the multiplication promise in verse 10. We could end up with the following:

And he will be a fruitful man,
his hand will be with all,
> and everyone's hand with him,

A CASE FOR THE POSSIBILITY OF CHANGING OUR MINDS

and before all his brothers he will dwell.

There are many layers that contribute to distrust and enmity between the Jews and Arabs, but a simple change of translation in this instance could soften some of those long-lasting tensions.[5]

New Testament interpretation example: *anathema*

The last book we covered in my old group Bible study (at Siloam Springs Bible Church, EFCA) was Paul's letter to the Galatians. I love this group because we were determined to focus on the text itself. We read aloud from various translations and then discussed what we heard with the benefit of a retired conservative Bible scholar (associated with John Brown University and Wycliffe Bible Translators) at the table who could help us with the original Greek text. My reading of Galatians 1:8-9 in New Testament scholar N.T. Wright's *Kingdom New Testament* translation (a favorite of our conservative scholar) is:

> "But even if we—or an angel from heaven!—should announce a gospel other than the one we proclaimed, let such a person be accursed. I said it before and I now say it again: if anyone offers you a gospel other than the one you received, let that person *be accursed.*
> — GALATIANS 1:8-9 (THE KINGDOM NEW TESTAMENT)

The various translations others were reading mostly said the same thing, translating the Greek word "anathema" (ἀνάθεμα 331) as "cursed by God" or "cursed" or "accursed." Yet one member's reading followed the New English Translation (NET)'s rendering of "let him be condemned to hell!" This conserva-

---

5 Interpretation/translation analysis indebted to Brian McLaren

tive scholarly translation, associated with Dallas Theological Seminary, decided to add a layer of meaning to Paul's words which may or may not have been his original intention. While it could be reasonable to interpret Paul's words as referring to eternal damnation, this is going beyond the actual literal text and applying a non-traditional interpretation as if it is the only way to read it. The 1984 NIV translation also interpreted this with added meaning as "eternally condemned", but the newer 2011 NIV removes the speculative timeframe with simply "under God's curse".

I'm not mentioning this only to pick on the NET Bible here (though I have noticed this is not the only place the translators of that version make similar decisions), but simply pointing out that some level of interpretation is a required and expected part of the translator's job.

Interpretation in reading and study

Of course, even after the texts are translated into English, different Christian communities can read them in different ways. We could dive into exhaustive discussion on this topic, but the simplest evidence that I know of is to point out that there are approximately 41,000 different denominations around the world that differentiate based on doctrine and practice for a variety of reasons. Every one of them believes that there was/is evidence, mostly from Scriptural sources, to insist on their interpretation being the best, if not the only, way of being Christian and reading the Bible.

One classic example within the evangelical community is the debate between Calvinism and Arminianism. This fundamental difference in how to read the Bible on the subjects of the nature of man, eternal predestination, and the extent of salvation has existed unresolved since the 17th century. Each side bases their positions on the teachings of a 16th century thelogian, respectively John Calvin or Jacobus Arminius. This debate continues to remain a distinctive split today, to the extend that some modern Calvinists claim that Arminianists aren't saved and/or preach heresy. For Calvin, what was key is that God has full and ultimate control over all aspects of the world and our lives:

> "I form the light and create darkness,
>   I bring prosperity and create disaster;
>   I, the LORD, do all these things."
>   — Isaiah 45:7

Subject	Calvinism	Arminianism
God's Sovereignty	God is in **absolute control** of every part of life, all good and evil according to his will.	God **limits his control** to give us freedom, though he knows what we will choose.
Ability to believe	We are **totally depraved** in our sin, requiring Spirit's regeneration to believe.	While fallen, we have **free will** to choose or reject salvation.
Predestination	God chose those he would save before creation **unconditionally**.	God **conditionally** chose only those whom he knew would freely believe in him.
Christ Atoned For	Christ's redemption was **limited** only to the elect, did not atone for all sinners.	Christ's atonement was **universal**, though we must choose to accept.
Call of the Spirit	The Spirit's call to salvation for the elect is **irresistible**.	We have free will to **resist** the drawing of the Spirit.
Assurance	The elect who are truly saved **persevere**—can never lose their salvation.	We can **fall from grace** if we do not continue in the faith.

Comparison chart of basic Calvinist vs Arminianist differences.

From this verse and similar ones, Calvinists claim that God predetermined and causes all things to happen for his own glory even though we may not understand them. This includes war, disease, famine, and poverty, in addition to all good things. Popular evangelical preachers in this vein include John Piper, Mark Driscoll, and John MacArthur.

Arminianists read these same verses differently because they see different aspects to God's character from Scripture. They point to Jesus's desire that all would be saved, and his weeping over Jerusalem as evidence that God gives us free will and the consequences which arise from our use of it. C.S. Lewis, Billy Graham and John Wesley would be examples of Arminianists.

For myself, I understand the Calvinist argument, but I don't agree with the interpretations of Scripture that it is based on for a variety of reasons. Therefore I do not agree with some of the core doctrines of many prominent, respected theologians and pastors like John Piper. Yet at the same time, I believe that John Piper is very intelligent, he loves God and people, he is devoted to his faith, and he does the best job he can to interpret the Bible accurately (and I freely admit he has more training and experience than I do). I must be humble enough to admit that I can never be certain I have chosen the "right" interpretation.

There are still other mainstream Protestant interpretations such as Anabaptists (e.g. Mennonites) or Lutherans. Once we add in Anglican, Roman Catholic and Eastern Orthodox perspectives, we end up with a vast variety of interpretations all based on the same written Scriptures.

Let's be clear. Within Christianity orthodoxy, even within just Evangelical Protestantism, we have interpretative disagreements on things as fundamental as:

1. Who did Jesus die for:
   - For God's needs or for humans'?
   - Limited to the elect only, or for all the world?
   - How does it save us, what atonement mechanism?
2. How then are you saved?
   - By belief alone? And on what belief?
   - What about the works which James discusses?
   - Must we persevere, or prove our transformation?
3. What about baptism forms, signs of the Spirit, which prayer do we use, can you lose your salvation, etc?

If these basic principles have so many orthodox interpretations from the same text, could we allow for the possibility of different interpretations on the subject of human sexuality? Does unity mean forced homogeny, or can it be a shared love both bridging and celebrating different perspectives?

> "I ask not only on behalf of these, but also on behalf of those who will believe in me through their word, that **they may all be one**. As you, Father, are in me and I am in you, may they also be in us, *so that the world may believe that you have sent me.* The glory that you have given me I have given them, so that **they may be one**, as we are one, I in them and you in me, that they may **become completely one**, *so that the world may know that you have sent me and have loved them even as you have loved me.*"
> — *Jesus speaking with his Father in* JOHN 17:20-23

This doesn't remove the need for critical reading of anyone making the case for a different interpretation of course. Please continue to do so.

Lessons from history for reading the Bible

Over the centuries, our churches have chosen positions on some social issues with which we no longer agree. These positions were supported by arguments directly from Scripture passages, and we can follow the same logic today as we read along with them. However, most conservative Evangelicals would find it very troubling to return to those same positions even though they had been in place for hundreds or thousands of years.

Here are a few examples, among many others:

- Geocentrism considered unambiguously supported by Scripture for 1,400 years until Copernicus and Galileo.
- The execution of heretics was supported by Saint Augustine and John Calvin among many others.
- "Manifest Destiny" justified the killing and oppression of native peoples in the Americas using Scriptural themes.
- American anti-abolitionism/pro-slavery was supported by conservative Christian preachers through the 1860s.
- Resistance to suffrage for nearly 100 years by appeal to Scripture.
- Antisemitism supported as ecumenical doctrine for nearly 2,000 years, until the Holocaust.
- Segregation supported by appeal to Scripture and Christianity through the 1960s, see Bob Jones, Sr.
- Interracial relationships and marriage prohibited on Biblical grounds as late as 2000 by Bob Jones University.
- Remarriage of divorcees prohibited without exception.

I'd like to highlight a few which may be helpful.

The geocentrism vs. heliocentrism debate: Copernicus and Galileo

In the 16th century, first Copernicus and then Galileo pushed back against the traditional and Biblically-supported view of the Earth-centered universe. Since Ptolemy published his work on astronomy in 150 CE, geocentrism had become accepted as the one valid explanation of our solar system. Resistance came from religious scholars who were convinced by the long-standing tradition (1,400 years) and their view that you could not hold the Scriptures to be infallible if you rejected geocentrism.

It was Protestant leaders who first pushed back on these new ideas of heliocentrism, as the Catholic Church initially had no concerns about the scientific research. Martin Luther was one who was opposed to this new theory, even before Copernicus' book was officially published:

> "There was mention of a certain new astrologer who wanted to prove that the earth moves and not the sky, the sun, and the moon. This would be as if somebody were riding on a cart or in a ship and imagined that he was standing still while the earth and the trees were moving. [Luther remarked] 'So it goes now. Whoever wants to be clever must agree with nothing that others esteem. He must do something of his own. This is what that fellow does who wishes to turn the whole of astronomy upside down. Even in these things that are thrown into disorder I believe the Holy Scriptures, for Joshua commanded the sun to stand still, and not the earth. [JOSHUA 10:12]'"
>
> — ATTRIBUTED TO MARTIN LUTHER IN *TABLE TALK*, 1539[6]

---

6 Martin Luther, *Luther's Works. Vol 54. Table Talk*, ed. Helmut T. Lehmann (Philadelphia: Fortress Press, 1967), 358–9.

Martin Luther also wrote that the literal descriptions of *stars fixed to the firmament with waters above them* were required to be held to with firm faith against those who wickedly denied them:

> "We Christians must be different from the philosophers [i.e. scientists] in the way we think about the causes of these things. And if some are beyond our comprehension (like those before us *concerning the waters above the heavens*), we must believe them and admit our lack of knowledge rather than either wickedly deny them or presumptuously interpret them in conformity with our understanding."
> — MARTIN LUTHER, *LECTURES IN GENESIS*[7]

Indeed, the descriptions of the "firmament" in Scripture are problematic in our modern understanding of the world. While it can be easy to read past this word as an archaic concept we don't understand, the original idea is quite simple. The world as described in the Hebrew Bible is founded on the model of the universe as depicted in the illustration to the left. The ancient Hebrews believed that there was a huge dome above the earth, upon which the stars were fixed and the sun travelled. This firmament separated the waters above and below the earth:

> And God said, "*Let there be a dome* in the midst of the waters, and let it separate the waters from the waters."
>
> So God made the dome and separated the *waters that were under the dome* from the *waters that were above the dome*. And it was so. God called the dome *Sky*.

---

7 Martin Luther, *Luther's Works. Vol 1. Lectures on Genesis*, ed. Jaroslav Pelikan (St. Louis: Concordia Publishing House, 1958), 30.

God made the two great lights—the greater light to rule the day and the lesser light to rule the night—and the stars. God *set them in the Dome of the sky* to give light upon the earth...

"...let birds fly above the earth *across the dome of the sky.*"
— Genesis 1:6-8a, 16-17, 20

We see this worldview repeated in the story of the flood, as God drew on the reserve waters out of which he had created the universe to make a world-ending flood a few chapters later:

...on that day all the *fountains of the great deep* burst forth, and the *windows of the heavens* were opened.
— Genesis 7:11b

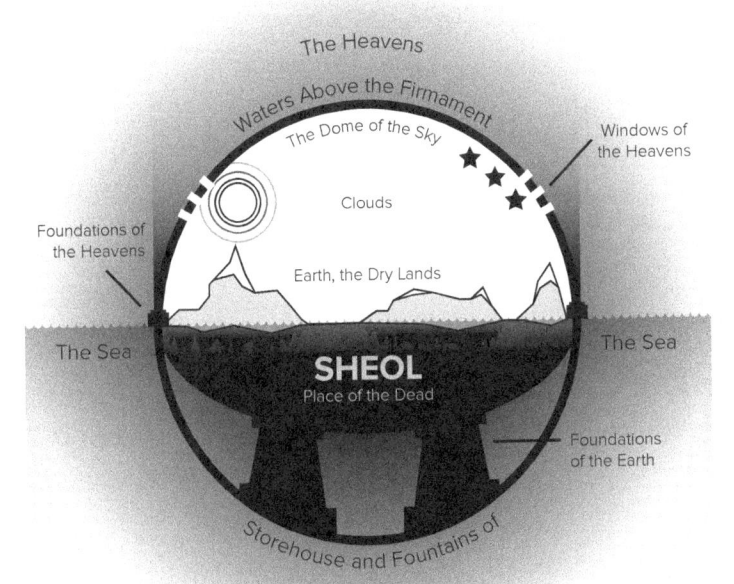

A literal dome, or "firmament", along with other aspects of this model is clearly described throughout the Bible. For example, verse 4 of Psalm 148 calls on the "*heavens of heavens* and *waters above the heavens*" to praise God.

By the time of the Reformation, the 2nd century CE astronomer Ptolemy's geocentric model of the universe was accepted by scientists and theologians alike. It had added some observations and mathematical models onto the older firmament view. Yet it was consistent with the foundational concept of the earth as the center of the universe, firmly planted in space while all else revolved around us in their own sets of nested spheres.

While Joshua stopping the movement of the sun was a primary text as Martin Luther pointed out, there were a number of other verses quoted in support of geocentrism. For example:

- "Surely the world is established, so that *it cannot be moved*." (PSALM 93:1B)
- "The world also is *firmly established*, it shall not be moved;" (PSALM 96:10 *and* 1 CHRONICLES 16:30B)
- "You who laid the *foundations of the world*, so that it should not be moved forever," (PSALM 104:5)
- "The *sun also rises, and the sun goes down*, and hastens to the place where it arose." (ECCLESIASTES 1:5)

In 1616, 67 years after Copernicus' book was originally published, the Catholic Church banned his work as heretical. They followed up with condemning Galileo as a heretic in 1633. The ban on Copernicus's work remained in place for two centuries while the debate gradually shifted toward acceptance of heliocentrism by both scientists and theologians. It was finally removed in 1822, while Galileo was only pardoned in 1992.

Today most Christians, even very conservative ones, have no concerns about reading these verses as poetry and not scientific descriptions. We might even think it ludicrous that the church would be bothered about this topic. Yet even today there are groups who insist that geocentrism must be the proper theory of astronomy by referencing these same verses.[8]

Solid Biblical support against the abolitionists

I trust we all find this horrifying today, but in the 1800's both sides of the Abolition debate were supported by ministers and Scriptural claims. Here is an excerpt out of one of the debates.

In 1860 the Reverend Henry J. Van Dyke wrote and preached a sermon in the First Presbyterian Church of Brooklyn titled "The Character and Influence of Abolitionism".[9] In this widely reprinted and distributed sermon he roundly denounced Abolitionists as abandoning Scripture:

> "...I am here to-night, in God's name, and by His help, to show that this tree of abolitionism is evil, and only evil, root and branch, flower and leaf, and fruit; that it springs from, and is nourished by, an utter rejection of the Scriptures; that it produces no real benefit to the enslaved, and is the fruitful source of division, and strife, and infidelity, in both church and State. I have four distinct propositions on the subject to maintain — four theses to nail up and defend:
>
> I. Abolitionism has no foundation in the Scriptures.
>
> II. Its principles have been promulgated chiefly by misrepresentation and abuse.

---

8 See Geocentricity.com or FixedEarth.com (citing 67 verses!) for example.

9 Read the sermon online at http://bit.ly/HS-VanDyke

> III. It leads, in multitudes of cases, and by a logical process, to utter infidelity.
>
> IV. It is the chief cause of the strife that agitates and the danger that threatens our country."
>
> — Reverend Henry Van Dyke (1860)

The Reverend Van Dyke goes on to cite Scriptures such as Genesis 17:23, 17:27, and Leviticus 25:44-46 (others include Deuteronomy 20:10-11, 1 Corinthians 7:21, Ephesians 6:1-5, Colossians 3:18-25; 4:1, and I Timothy 6:1-2). He speaks of Jesus' silence on the subject of slavery in the gospels, when he would have been surrounded by Roman slavery. He refers to verses in the Epistles mentioned above which instruct good treatment of slaves and obedience to masters, but do not condemn slavery. He expresses his fears that the proponents of abolitionism are forcing the division of the nation in their fervor.

The last point above has some resonance in our debates today. Both James Dobson and Alan Keyes, prominent and politically-influential conservative Christians, argued that a summer 2015 Supreme Court decision in favor of same-sex marriage could bring us to a new civil war.

The Reverend J. R. W. Sloane published a review and refutation of Van Dyke's sermon shortly after it was preached, which shows that not all agreed with this anti-Abolitionist position but neither was it an isolated outlier in the debate at the time:

> "Were the author of the discourse some obscure or eccentric individual, without position and without character, we might pass it by in silence, leaving it to the scorn of the Christian world, and the oblivion to which it must ultimately be consigned. When we consider, however, that he is a minister,

said to be a man of intellect and of culture, pastor of a large and respectable congregation in a neighboring city, occupying an important and responsible position in a religious denomination which is one of the most powerful and influential in the country, the cause of truth and righteousness demands a different mode of treatment. We are to remember, also, that the principles which he advocates are those of the Old School Presbyterian Church, with which he is connected; that his sentiments, however abhorrent to all right Christian feeling, are thundered from hundreds of pulpits Sabbath after Sabbath by men who are the chosen moral and religious teachers of the people — men, too, by no means contemptible or to be despised.

It may be said that I do injustice, when I charge upon an ecclesiastical body the sentiments of a solitary individual connected with it. To this, I reply that the Rev. Mr. Van Dyke claims that these are the principles of his Church, and no one has ventured to deny the claim."

— Reverend J. R. W. Sloane (1861)[10]

The most troubling discovery I found is the claim that it was easier for the pro-slavery ministers to make their case from Scripture than it was for the abolitionists. The plain, simple reading of the verses clearly did not protest against slavery, and readings that tried to look for the spirit of the law rather than the letter were accused of twisting the truth.

---

10 *Review of Rev. Henry J. Van Dyke's discourse on "The character and influence of abolitionism," a sermon preached in the Third Reformed Presbyterian Church, Twenty-third Street, New York, on Sabbath evening, December 23, 1860* by J. R. W. Sloane

Leaders of the Southern Baptist Convention (SBC), the largest Protestant denomination in America, have publicly described their stance against same-sex marriage with the words *"We are on the wrong side of history, just like we started."*[11] Yet they were formed in 1845 by a denominational split over slavery—choosing to separate so as to appoint slaveholders as ministers and missionaries against a ruling of the national Baptist Board. The official complaint listed in the formation Proceedings[12] was that slaveholders were not being treated as equals in the church by their Northern counterparts. Baptist theology in the region had undergone a dramatic pro-slavery shift after a few decades of strong church growth.

The first president of the South Carolina State Baptist Convention, the Rev. Richard Furman, wrote in 1823:

> "...the sentiments in opposition to the holding of slaves have been attributed, by their advocates, to the Holy Scriptures, and to the genius of Christianity. These sentiments, the Convention...cannot think just, or well-founded: for the right of holding slaves is clearly established by the Holy Scriptures, both by precept and example."

He described how the Law in the Tanakh regulated permanent and inheritable slave ownership of certain people based on their tribal origin (Leviticus 25:44-46). Paul's letters to Timothy in the New Testament clearly instruct slaves to *"regard their masters as worthy of all honor, so that the name of God and the teaching may not be blasphemed"* (1 Timothy 6:1b).

---

11 "Why the church should neither cave nor panic about the decision on gay marriage," The Washington Post, Russell Moore, June 2015

12 "Proceedings of the Southern Baptist Convention, 1845," Baylor Archives

Furman continued his argument in support of slavery by appealing to Divine Law and morality:

> "Had the holding of slaves been a moral evil, it cannot be supposed, that the inspired Apostles, who feared not the faces of men, and were ready to lay down their lives in the cause of their God, would have tolerated it, for a moment, in the Christian Church. ...they let the relationship remain untouched, as being lawful and right, and insist on the relative duties.
>
> In proving this subject justifiable by Scriptural authority, its morality is also proved; for the Divine Law never sanctions immoral actions."[13]

It was another 150 years before the denomination made an official statement of regret and apology for their historic support of slavery, racism, and segregation.[14]

On this side of the debate, we can rejoice in knowing that there were many convicted, inspired white Christians like Anglican William Wilberforce, Presbyterian Charles Finny, and Quaker Benjamin Lay who worked hard to overturn slavery. We should not blame Christians or the Bible solely for the institution of slavery, or for the 450 years it existed in America based on an appeal to racial inferiority. However, it is important to recognize the responsibility that a widely accepted interpretation of the Bible had in giving support to the institution for many centuries.

---

13 "Rev. Dr. Richard Furman's EXPOSITION of The Views of the Baptists, RELATIVE TO THE COLOURED POPULATION In the United States IN A COMMUNICATION To the Governor of South-Carolina", 2nd edition, 1938.

14 "Resolution On Racial Reconciliation On The 150th Anniversary Of The Southern Baptist Convention", 1995

Universal support for antisemitism

Another tragic mis-interpretation of Scripture can be found in near-universal church support for antisemitism from the first century until after World War II. It's hard for many of us today to fathom that this was true because it's not something we have experienced in our lifetimes. Support from 2,000 years of tradition, church leaders, and specific verses in Scripture had Protestant, Catholic and Orthodox churches united against the Jews as a cursed race, to be completely replaced by the church in God's plan.

Verses such as Matthew 8:12 and 18:31-33, John 8:43-47, and I Thessalonians 2:14-16 were read as God's condemnation of the Jewish people as a whole. One of the strongest passages used was Matthew's account of *"the people as a whole"*, the Jews, accepting full responsibility for Christ's death on themselves and their children (interpreted as all descendants):

> So when Pilate saw that he could do nothing, but rather that a riot was beginning, he took some water and washed his hands before the crowd, saying, "I am innocent of this man's blood; see to it yourselves."
>
> Then the people as a whole answered, *"His blood be on us and on our children!"*
>
> So he released Barabbas for them; and after flogging Jesus, he handed him over to be crucified.
> — MATTHEW 27:24-26

Many Christian leaders from the first centuries on taught that Scripture taught the condemnation of the Jew and Judaism:

"...they have committed a crime of the most unhallowed kind, in conspiring against the savior" and "The blood of Jesus falls not only on the Jews of that time, but on all generations of Jews up to the end of the world."
— ORIGEN (C.A. 200 CE)

"Judaism is a corruption. Indeed Judas is the image of the Jewish people. Their understanding of the Scriptures is carnal. They bear the guilt for the death of the saviour, for through their fathers they have killed the Christ."
— ST. AGUSTINE (C.A. 400 CE)

"Jews are slayers of the Lord, murderers of the prophets, enemies of God, haters of God, adversaries of grace, enemies of their fathers' faith, advocates of the devil, brood of vipers, slanderers, scoffers, men of darkened minds, leaven of the Pharisees, congregation of demons, sinners, wicked men, stoners and haters of goodness."
— ST. GREGORY (C.A. 600 CE)

By the end of his life, the great reformer Martin Luther had switched from a supporter of the Jews to a strong antisemitic. He wrote a book called *"On the Jews and Their Lies"* in which he urged for the destruction of homes and synagogues, forbidding religious teaching, confiscation of valuables (until they convert to Christianity), forced labor, and eviction from the country. At one time he wrote "...we are at fault in not slaying them...", which had an enormous impact 400 years later in the Lutheran churches of Germany.

Based on these teachings Adolf Hitler confidently proclaimed in *Mein Kampf*: "I believe that I am today acting according to the purposes of the Almighty Creator. In resisting the Jew, I am fighting the Lord's battle." In a speech addressing Polish Catholics he stated "I as a German Catholic, ask only what is permitted to Polish Catholics. To be antisemitic is not to be un-Catholic. The Church used every weapon against the Jews, even the Inquisition. Christ himself was a pioneer in the fight against Judaism."

Dr. David Gushee, an evangelical Southern Baptist scholar specializing in Holocaust study and Christian Ethics, writes that during World War II some Jews seeking help from Christians were met with explanations of why they would not be helped, supported by passages in the Bible and from the writings of early church fathers. It took a willingness to look past church teachings and see people in need for help to be given.

Fortunately, the church felt forced to go back to those Scriptures after being confronted with the horror of the Holocaust. In 1965 the Catholic Church officially reversed their original teaching that all Jews were responsibility for Christ's death. Within a short period most churches changed their interpretations of what had appeared to be very clear verses for nearly 2,000 years. Sadly, there are still some conservative churches in America who teach that the Jews are an eternally cursed race, and much of anti-semitism is still supported by an appeal to Scripture.[15]

---

15 For more, see Dr. Gushee's research found in *Changing Our Minds* or online at http://www.reformationproject.org/gushee-endingcontempt

Can those who are divorced remarry and stay in the church?

Let's look at one last small example. Traditionally churches have agreed that Scripture clearly taught (Mark 10:10-12) that all divorced people, regardless of fault or reason, were banned from remarriage (see the Appendix for more). Since the person they had been married to was still living, it was considered to be a form of ongoing adultery, not just a one-time problem. This current theological argument about the difference between a single committed sin and living in ongoing sinful practices is applied today against same-sex marriage.

Popular lay Anglican theologian C.S. Lewis ran into this barrier and successfully countered it in ways that might apply to this current topic. In 1957 the Church of England refused to marry C.S. Lewis and Joy Davidman because she was divorced (her husband divorced her for leaving America years after he abandoned the family due to alcoholism and affairs). One local parish priest decided to marry them anyway after the Bishop of Oxford turned them down. It wasn't until 2002, 45 years later, that the Church of England officially changed policies to allow remarriage under certain conditions.

Today, churches interpret the same Scriptures on this subject in different ways, as the examples show below:

Forbidden	Limited	Allowed
Reformed Presbyterian	Evangelical Presbyterian	Presbyterian (USA)
Southern Baptist	American Baptist	United Methodists
Roman Catholic	Church of England	Episcopal
	Lutheran (Missouri)	Lutheran (ELCA)
	Evangelical Free	

Why is there so much pain in the LGBT community?

We'll now move on to the third section of this chapter, looking at the painful experiences of the LGBT community.

There is much which can be written and debated on this topic. What cannot be denied however is the extent of pain and damage being experienced among those in the lesbian, gay, bisexual and transgender (LGBT) communities.

Suicide, depression and abuse

It's widely accepted that people in these groups suffer from depression, substance abuse, and suicide at higher rates than the average population. A number of studies have shown that lesbian, gay and bisexual youth have a **four times greater rate of attempting suicide** (up to 40% of the kids).

These rates increase dramatically when they face strong family rejection, doubling the suicide rate again to eight times normal. Even though the estimate of the gay population is roughly 5% of the country, gay youth make up **40% of the homeless youth population** overall due to being kicked out of their homes.[16]

22% of them don't feel safe at school (compared to 7% of the non-gay population). 90% (vs 62%) are harrassed or assaulted each year. The "...higher prevalence of suicidal ideation and overall mental health problems...has been attributed to minority stress" according to an article on Wikipedia.

We can see ripple effects from the harshest conservative Christian advocates against homosexuality around the world. In 2009 three evangelical American Christian activists partici-

---

[16] According to the "LGBT Homeless Youth Provider Survey", 2012

pated in a conference that advocated against homosexuality in Uganda, leading to a bill proposing a unilateral death penalty for all gay people regardless of practice. After modification to a sentence of life imprisonment, this was passed in 2014. Even though it is currently held up in the courts, the discussion led to increased violence against gay and lesbian people in the country. Jeffery Gettleman for the New York Times writes: "Human rights advocates in Uganda say the visit by the three Americans helped set in motion what could be a very dangerous cycle. Gay Ugandans already describe a world of beatings, blackmail, death threats like 'Die Sodomite!' scrawled on their homes, constant harassment and even so-called correctional rape." [17]

What is the cause of these problems?

There are two general ideas about why there are so many mental and physical problems amongst the LGBT population. The first is the view many conservative Christians hold. The second is offered as a possible alternative or supplement:

1. **Homosexuality is a sin and there are consequences.** The conservative Christian understanding of homosexuality (orientation and/or practice, depending) is that it is a sin, and that those who live in sin face both temporal and eternal consequences. They may not recognize a societal and cultural component to the suffering. Some would say that the consequences should include marginalization and exclusion from Christian fellowship until they conform to traditional doctrine.

---

[17] "Americans' Role Seen in Uganda Anti-Gay Push", Jeffery Gettleman, 2010
http://www.nytimes.com/2010/01/04/world/africa/04uganda.html

2. **The marginalization and abuse of gay people is causing the issues.** Another perspective is to wonder if the attitudes and actions of the surrounding culture is contributing to the problem. When conservative Christian organizations and individuals make very clear their belief that God rejects homosexuals and/or their experience of love, and this is reinforced by much of our culture to the point of parents rejecting their own kids in turn, it seems reasonable that this could directly impact a person's sense of their self and how God's love applies (or not) to them.

If there is even a small possibility of the second option having some responsibility for the problems, it seems that we should take this very seriously and make some extra effort to be sure that we're getting it right.

As a quick example before we move on, what if we were to consider the potential outcomes to a decision to suspend judgement and remain completely silent on this issue? Even if the traditional "non-affirming" argument is correct, then we would be leaving it to the Holy Spirit to convict our brothers and sisters as they grow in faith and maturity in Christ. The downside of continued vocal opposition being wrong may be considered far more damaging.

A short personal account

I found this relevant excerpt from the book by Dr. Gushee talking about how he changed his mind:

> "My beloved baby sister, Katey, a single mother and a Christian, who had been periodically hospitalized with depression and

anxiety, including one suicide attempt, came out as a lesbian in 2008. Her testimony is that her depression was largely caused by her inability to even acknowledge her sexuality, let alone integrate it with her faith – and this was largely caused by the Christian teaching she had received. The fact that traditionalist Christian teaching produces despair in just about every gay or lesbian person who must endure is surely very relevant information for the LGBT debate."

Fragmentation and Rejection of the Church

We face two large crises in our churches today as well.

Fragmentation of unity

Because this issue is often viewed as one that we cannot "agree to disagree" on, we are facing church and denomination splits. The Episcopal church division in 2007 was one of the most high-profile, with some more conservative congregations deciding that they could not remain in fellowship with colleagues they were officially free to disagree with. Many joined with Anglican congregations in Nigeria or other parts of Africa in an attempt to remain part of the Anglican union without assocating with their fellow churches in this country (although these conservative groups are no longer officially recognized as part of the Church by the Archbishop of Canterbury, according to the rules that govern the Anglican Communion).

I am reminded of Jesus's words to his disciples, that we be known by our unity (not by how much we agree). It is sad to see how this core identity seems to be disappearing. If there is even a chance that we could remain in community together, shouldn't we seek that possibility?

Rejection of the church by the younger generation

As these social issues seem to becoming the main focus of the conservative Christian community in the United States, the younger generation appears to be repelled more and more by the representation of the Gospel that they are seeing. While we should never give up truth to be popular, what if we are wrong and our witness is driving people away from the hope of Christ? What if the unpopular truth is for our own community, in a parallel with Christ's condemnation of the religious elite of his day?

A 2007 survey of 16-29 year-olds by evangelical Christian research organization Barna Group found:

Non-Christian 16-29 year-olds:

- Only 16% have a "good impression" of Christianity, down from a majority a decade ago.
- Only 3% expressed favorable views of evangelicals, down from 25% favorable views from Boomers.
- Top negative perceptions:
    - judgmental (87%)
    - hypocritical (85%)
    - old-fashioned (78%)
    - too involved in politics (75%)
- 91% describe Christianity as primarily "anti-homosexual"

Church-going 16-29 year-old Christians:

- Half also perceive Christianity to be judgmental, hypocritical, and too political.

A CASE FOR THE POSSIBILITY OF CHANGING OUR MINDS

- One-third said it was old-fashioned and out of touch with reality.
- 80% believe Christianity can be described as "anti-homosexual"

The report continues with some commentary:

"...non-Christians and Christians explained that beyond their recognition that Christians oppose homosexuality, they believe that Christians show excessive contempt and unloving attitudes towards gays and lesbians. One of the most frequent criticisms of young Christians was that they believe the church has made homosexuality a 'bigger sin' than anything else. Moreover, they claim that the church has not helped them apply the biblical teaching on homosexuality to their friendships with gays and lesbians.

"When young people were asked to identify their impressions of Christianity, one of the common themes was 'Christianity is changed from what it used to be' and 'Christianity in today's society no longer looks like Jesus.' These comments were the most frequent unprompted images that young people called to mind, mentioned by one-quarter of both young non-Christians (23%) and born again Christians (22%)."[18]

Another survey[19] shows that the abandonment of the church is increasing with these younger generations who are also generally much more supportive of gay marriage:

---

18 https://www.barna.org/barna-update/teens-nextgen/94-a-new-generation-expresses-its-skepticism-and-frustration-with-christianity (2007)

19 https://www.barna.org/barna-update/culture/685-five-trends-among-the-unchurched (2014)

"Nearly half of Millennials (48%) qualify as post-Christian

Percentage of Americans qualifying as post-Christian

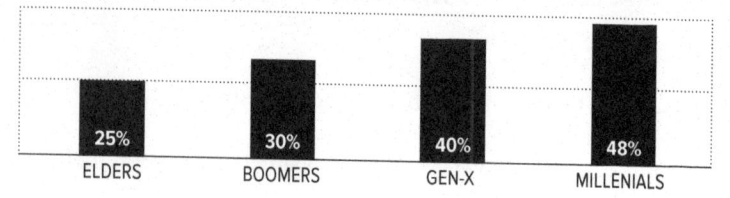

ELDERS	BOOMERS	GEN-X	MILLENIALS
25%	30%	40%	48%

compared to two-fifths of Gen-Xers (40%), one-third of Boomers (35%) and one-quarter of Elders (28%)."

Among those who no longer go to church:

"...almost half (49%) could not identify a single favorable impact of the Christian community, while nearly two-fifths (37%) were unable to identify a negative impact. Of those who could identify one way Christians contribute to the common good, the unchurched appreciate their influence when it comes to serving the poor and disadvantaged (22%), bolstering morals and values (10%) and helping people believe in God (8%). Among those who had a complaint about Christians in society, the unchurched were least favorably disposed toward violence in the name of Christ (18%), **the church's stand against gay marriage (15%)**, sexual abuse scandals (13%) and involvement in politics (10%)."

What if we are incorrect on our judgement against homosexuality and this is causing direct harm to our representation of Christ in our world? Again, shouldn't we take the time to prayerfully consider our position very carefully given the negative effects to the perception of church in our society?

Conclusion

Nothing in this section should suggest that we must change our minds on the topic. However, I hope that it is clear how there may be a possibility of changing our minds, and how important it is to be sure that we are correct if we are going to continue wholesale rejection of homosexuality. There is much at stake for our churches, our communities, and for all people created in the image of God in our country and around the world.

If you're willing to continue this journey into what our Bible has to say on the subject, I hope you'll join me in an earnest exploration of six key passages in the following chapters.

*"But before they lay down, the men of the city,
the men of Sodom, both young and old,
all the people to the last man,
surrounded the house;
and they called to Lot,
'Where are the men who came to you tonight?
Bring them out to us, so that we may know them.'"*
— Genesis 19:4-5

CHAPTER 3
The Tale of Sodom and Gomorrah

The story of the destruction of the cities of Sodom and Gomorrah has long been associated with sex between men in the lore of our Western culture. The term "sodomy" and the label "sodomite" are derived directly from the city named in the 19th chapter of Genesis. We turn to this passage first in our exploration of the Bible and homosexuality because of its early chronological position in Scripture, the foundations it gives us for further discussion, and also because it's one of the most straight-forward passages to study.

I will start each of our study sections with questions which will form the structure of each discussion. You may not agree with some of the answers I suggest, but I hope you'll find the process valuable and illuminating anyway.

Here are the questions we'll seek to answer in this chapter:

1. What happened in Sodom, and why?
2. What can we learn from how this episode is referenced throughout the Bible?
3. What can this teach us about how ancient people viewed the genders and sex?

The sin of Sodom

First, let's look at our primary text, Genesis 19, within the Scriptural and historical context. Then we'll take a look at a few other passages that reference the topic.

Background on the cities of Sodom and Gomorrah

Our story starts with Abraham. He has settled in the region of Canaan, in Hebron, after his nephew Lot chooses the fertile, wealthy plain near the Jordan filled with cities. Lot pitches his tent near Sodom, filled with people described as *"...wicked, great sinners against the Lord."* (GENESIS 13:13) Archeologists don't agree on exactly where the original city might have been situated, but the assumption is that it was near what we now call the Dead Sea. This would put it in the Jordan Rift Valley near significant amounts of flammable gas, sulfur and asphalt.

While our primary narrative is in the 19th chapter, we can gain some more background knowledge about the twin cities of Sodom and Gomorrah in a previous chapter. This gives us insight into what the cities are known for.

In chapter 14, nephew Lot is caught up in the conquest of kings as a number of rulers rebel against others and war ensues. Sodom is on the losing end, and all the people are captured—presumably to be slaves. Abraham gathers his allies in the area, pursues the enemy army, and brings everyone back. After a special blessing from the priest Melchizedek, the king of Sodom offers to let Abraham keep all the looted goods in exchange for allowing all the people to return home. Abraham rejects this offer, wanting nothing to do with wealth from this "wicked city". I wonder—was the wealth tainted in Abraham's eyes because it came from slavery? You could even read this as Abraham being offered a slave purchase price, instead of being given a generous gift in thankfulness. After all, it's the possession of the people that the king of Sodom seems to want most.

Speculation aside, it seems clear that Abraham is well aware of Sodom and the sins of its people. By turning down the offered goods, Abraham is keeping his independence from the rulers of Sodom. He ensures that there will not be any obligations between the two parties that could be used against him in the future. We don't know exactly what the sins were at this point in the narrative other than something very much opposed to God.

Setting the scene

In chapters 15-17 we see God reiterating his promises to Abraham, while Ishmael is born and hope for an heir through Sarai is waning.

Immediately before the Sodom narrative, we hear of a special visit. Abraham has travelled to the Terebinths of Mamre from his home base of Hebron. The Amorite king named Mamre was one of Abraham's primary allies in rescuing Lot just a few chapters ago (Genesis 14:24). His seat of residence was known then (and for hundreds of years after, until the time of Roman Emperor Constantine around 300 CE) for being the site of one of the big three festivals in the region. It was likely a big trade fair for the region, and was often associated with cult worship of the Canaanite chief god of the sky known as El. Maybe Abraham was in town for resupplying, or selling some of his herds, or just visiting friends?

As Abraham seeks the shade of his tent in the heat of the day, he sees three strangers approach. This could have been quite common in Mamre, maybe in contrast to the remote regions where he would often find himself in his nomadic travels for pasture for his herds. Bear in mind that Abraham is described as very wealthy, and he's a close ally of the local king. He's not a lowly shepherd, that's for sure.

Yet as soon as Abraham sees these men, he runs over to them, bows low, and begs them to give him the honor of serving them. He describes himself as a *"servant"*, and offers to bring them water to wash with, a resting place under the tree, and *"a little bread"*. When they accept, he scurries around, asking Sarai to personally make cakes with the best flour (she likely had servants for most ordinary meal preparation), choosing a calf to be slaughtered by his servants, and bringing out curds and milk. This is quite a welcome for complete strangers! Abraham is demonstrating both the kind of Middle Eastern hospitality that was and is still held in high regard, and his servant heart that God values.

Why is this important? As we'll see next, Abraham's actions are soon held up in strong contrast.

Arriving in the city of Sodom

Skipping quickly through the prophecies, Sarai's laugh, and Abraham begging God to reconsider judgement of the cities, we arrive with the "messengers" (now known to be angels) at the gates of the city of Sodom. Here they meet Lot who urges them to come to his house for lodging and food instead of staying the night in the city square.

After a meal, they are getting ready to sleep (night is falling) when *"the men of Sodom, both young and old, all the people to the last man"* (GENESIS 19:4) surrounded the house and insisted that the strangers be brought out so that they could *"know"* them. The Hebrew word *yada* (עֲדִי 3045) here translated as *"know"* is mostly used for learning, knowledge or abilities, but is sometimes a euphemism for sexual intimacy as in Genesis 4:1.

Lot begs for protection for his guests, insisting that they are under his roof and his responsibility. He offers his daughters to the crowd in exchange for the men which likely confirms the idea of sex being involved somehow. Not only is this rejected, but the crowd says *"This fellow came here as an alien [referring to a temporary resident, not a citizen], and he would play the judge! Now we will deal worse with you than with them."* (GENESIS 19:9)

The story continues with rescue, blindness, escape, and destruction. It leads to another crisis in which Lot's daughters resort to incest to continue their family line after their mother is killed, which I mention in relation to a coming parallel account. We are left with this episode as a demonstration of the wickedness of the city of Sodom that leads to its destruction.

So, what exactly is the sin of Sodom? It may seem obvious now, but let's take a closer look.

A parallel story in Judges 19

Before we move on to some responses to that question taken from other Scripture references, I think it's useful to look at another story that has a lot of parallels with this one. We can find it in Judges 19.

You may be familiar with this quite disturbing story from the period between the exodus and the establishment of the kingdom of Israel. It starts with a member of the tribe of Levi, the tribe of priests who live among the other tribes' territories. This man takes a concubine (a second wife, "*pilegesh*") from Bethlehem back to his home in Ephraim. At some point they quarrel ("*[she] became angry with him*") to the extent that she returns home to Bethlehem. Four months later, he sets out after her, "*to speak tenderly to her and bring her back*". After a warm welcome and three-day-long feast—note the excessive hospitality at the beginning of the story, similar to Abraham's treatment of guests—the Levite sets off for his home with the woman late in the day, ignoring his father-in-law's plea to wait until the following morning.

As night fell they found themselves near Jerusalem. While this city is later known as the City of David, at this point it was controlled by a non-Israelite tribe called the Jebusites. The Levite dismisses his servant's advice to stop here in favor of finding a town owned by a fellow Israelite tribe (just as in Jesus' parable of the good Samaritan our assumptions about "our neighbors" are often wrong). They eventually stop in the town square of a Benjamite town called Gibeah, but find no hospitality until one old man offers to house them. As in the story of Lot, this old man is a temporary resident from another tribe and not an official citizen of the tribe of Benjamin.

Once again, the men of the town surround the house demanding sex with the Levite. Once again, the host offers two women to the mob—his virgin daughter and the Levite's concubine. The crowd *"would not listen to him"* (JUDGES 19:25). However, in this story the Levite grabs his concubine and pushes her outside to the men who rape and abuse her all night. At dawn she returns and falls on the threshold of the host's house, and is found there, apparently unconscious or dead, by her husband. He reacts with by saying: *"Get up, we are going."* When she doesn't answer, he loads her onto the back of a donkey and heads out of town.

In one of the most gruesome accounts in the Bible, the Levite takes the woman's body home, cuts it into pieces, and sends it around the tribes to ask for vengeance against the Benjamites. The invitation is so enthusiastically and effectively accepted that they nearly wipe the tribe out. This leads to yet another crisis of heredity, and another disturbing story of mass destruction and rape which could have something to say about the failure of trying to solve violence with more violence.

When the Levite gives his testimony of the crimes of the people of Gibeah before the battle with the Benjamites, he describes the events and motives very differently than we might have thought:

> *They intended to kill me,*
> *and they raped my concubine until she died.*
> —JUDGES 20:5

Note that the man did not seem worried about being raped, but about being killed! He saw the actions of the crowd being about a desire for violence and not about sexual desire.

Now, how does this compare to the much earlier account in Genesis? To highlight the parallels between the two stories, I've compiled details of the events in a comparison table below:

Event	**Sodom** (Genesis 19)	**Gibeah** (Judges 19)
Protagonists:	Two angels	Levite and concubine
Previous generous host:	Abraham	Father-in-law
City of event:	Sodom (Canaanite)	Gibeah (Israelite)
Seeking hospitality in:	Town square	Town square
Who offers hospitality?	Lot (resident alien)	Old man (resident alien)
Request of residents:	"we may 'know' them"	"we may have intercourse with him"
Counter-offer by host:	Virgin daughters	Virgin daughter and concubine
Reaction of town:	Host threatened as outsider	Only interested in outsider concubine
End of encounter:	Men struck blind by angels	Concubine raped and killed
Final judgement:	Cities destroyed	Tribe (nearly) destroyed
Genetic line continues:	Through incest	Through kidnapping & rape

Now that we can see how strong so many of the parallels are, I think it's valid to assume we can apply some observations back and forth between the stories. We might learn more about the culture and practices of the time that give insight to our main questions.

The Benjamite mob reject the offer of women from the host, but are satisfied with raping (and killing!) a visiting woman instead of a man. Must the motivation be solely same-gender sexual desire, or is it something else?

The Levite testifies that *"they intended to kill me."* Is it possible this is about extreme inhospitality—violence against strangers in the town—instead of sexual desire?

Summary analysis of our stories

Before we look further into the Scriptures for more insight into these events, let's look back at the Genesis and Judges texts one more time. There are a few points worth considering.

It's important to remember that the judgement of Sodom and Gomorrah is declared well before the angels are threatened in Genesis 19, and it goes back to descriptions of the cities' behaviors in previous chapters (it's not likely that this is a predictive-judgement when the angels talk to Abraham). We can likely only see the events recorded here as symptoms or examples of at least part of why the judgement is given. We may learn more about this from other verses in the Bible that reference this event and the sins, which is coming up next.

Abraham and Lot's hospitality and provision for strangers is contrasted with the rest of the city-dwellers of Sodom. This is the same for the Levite's experience with his father-in-law in a city of Judea and with a fellow Ephraimite, compared to his treatment in a city of Israel.

Every male person in Sodom is described as coming to Lot's door, not a smaller subset of the population (current modern estimates say that roughly 90-95% of people are naturally heterosexual). In Judges, it's not all the men, but they are equally satisfied with raping a woman.

Also notice that Lot offers his daughters up to be raped! This is how seriously he takes his responsibility to care for absolute

THE TALE OF SODOM AND GOMORRAH 57

strangers under his roof. Unfortunately, this also gives us a hint about how women were valued in his culture as well. We see this dismissive attitude toward women even more strongly in how the Levite treats his concubine in Judges 19.

The men of the city seem to have something against Lot as a temporary resident, instead of a citizen. In Judges, again only the "outsider" takes in the outsiders.

Finally, the timing of the events in both stories brings another story to mind that's a little closer to home. Both sets of visitors in town are safe until sundown, but not welcome afterward. My hometown of Siloam Springs, Arkansas is also the home of my alma-mater, the evangelical Christian college John Brown University. It was founded in 1919 by an evangelist as a place to instill conservative Christian values in the head, heart and hands of its students. Another thing that Siloam Springs prided itself on in that same year, as shown in the flyer below, is the lack of "Malaria, Mosquitos, and Negroes". It was one of Arkansas' Sundown Towns where all African Americans were told to leave

Postcard advertising the benefits of Siloam Springs, AR in 1919

before sunset or risk lynching. It is a sobering reminder of the violent exclusion of "outsiders" in our very recent past.

Now that we've thoroughly covered the original events in Sodom and Gomorrah, and compared the parallel account in Judges, it's time to move on and see if we can learn more from references to the cities in other areas of Scripture.

Finding Sodom throughout the Bible

The events in Sodom are a popular reference point throughout the Bible as an example of the consequences of sin. I found 18 verses in the Tanakh, and 10 in the New Testament, that contain the city name of "Sodom". They can be grouped into 12 topics, as shown here:

1. The completion of the giving of the law (DEUTERONOMY)
2. The prophecies of Isaiah (CHAPTERS 1, 3 AND 13)
3. The prophecies of Jeremiah (CHAPTERS 23, 49, 50)
4. The prophecies of Ezekiel (CHAPTER 16)
5. The fourth Lamentation (CHAPTER 4)
6. Indictment of the proud women in the book of Amos (CHAPTER 4)
7. Moab and the Ammonites condemned (ZEPHANIAH)
8. Jesus sends out the disciples, with warnings (MATTHEW, MARK AND LUKE)
9. Paul references Isaiah (ROMANS)
10. Peter reassures the tempted faithful (2 PETER)
11. A warning of sins and judgement (JUDE)
12. Rejection of God's messengers (REVELATION)

Now, let's work briefly through each of these references to see what we can learn.

Deuteronomy: a warning to Israel at the end of the giving of the law

> "...all its soil burned out by sulfur and salt, nothing planted,
> nothing sprouting, unable to support any vegetation,
> like the destruction of Sodom and Gomorrah, Admah and
> Zeboiim, which the Lord destroyed in his fierce anger."
> — Deuteronomy 29:23

In the first reference, we see Moses warning the people to follow God lest they end up like Sodom and Gomorrah. In context, he's closing all the instructions in the book of Deuteronomy with this vivid lesson. He seems to be emphasizing the temptation of idol worship specifically in this warning.

In the second reference in Deuteronomy a few chapters later (Deuteronomy 32:32) the abandonment of Yahweh worship for idolatry and demon worship is clearly compared to what was produced by Sodom, as poisonous grapes from a vineyard.

Isaiah: the nation of Israel compared to Sodom and Gomorrah

> "Hear the word of the Lord,
> you rulers of Sodom!
> Listen to the teaching of our God,
> you people of Gomorrah!"
> — Isaiah 1:10

Throughout the first chapter of the book of the prophet Isaiah, we see that the nation of Judah (Israel is already conquered and deported) is compared to the people of Sodom and Gomorrah. The direct reference is named in verses 9 and 10—the center of the argument. Along with this comparison we find two sets of specifics from God—things he condemns that they are doing, and things he wants from them.

1. **Abandon:** Your sacrifices to God of blood and burning flesh, all incense and offerings (*"who asked this from your hand?"* in verse 12), celebrations of Sabbath and appointed festivals (*"they have become a burden to me"* in verse 14), and all prayers (*"I will not listen"* in verse 15).
2. **Begin:** *"Wash yourselves; make yourselves clean; remove the evil of your doings from before my eyes; cease to do evil, learn to do good; seek justice, rescue the oppressed, defend the orphan, plead for the widow."* (ISAIAH 1:16-17)

The passage continues in a further comparison of Jerusalem to a female prostitute, accusing the inhabitants of greed, bribery, and injustice toward orphans and widows (the powerless and marginalized of society) in Isaiah 1:21-23. Note how directly traditional worship, prayer and observing the law are rejected in favor of caring for the vulnerable!

In the second mention of the city we see that Judah is being compared to Sodom in the way they brag of their sins: *"they proclaim their sin like Sodom, they do not hide it"* (ISAIAH 3:9). As we read the surrounding context of this verse to see what those sins are, we find that they are judged for:

> "It is you who have devoured the vineyard;
> the spoil of the poor is in your houses.
> What do you mean by crushing my people,
> by grinding the face of the poor?"
> — ISAIAH 3:14-15

Then the pride issue is repeated—the *"daughters of Zion are haughty"* (Isaiah 3:16)—with a description that sounds like the "daughters" in our example are flaunting their wealth (with *"tinkling"* ankle jewelry) and position in the face of those of their own people whom they are oppressing for greed.

Finally, we see the third reference to Sodom in Isaiah 13:19 being used to predict the destruction of Babylon. There are no clear hints directly in the text about a specific kind of sin being to blame. We can likely infer that the readers of this book would immediately be thinking about the forced exile (foreigners in a foreign land, likely in some form of enslavement) they were under at the time.

Jeremiah condemns Jerusalem, Edom and Babylon

> "But in the prophets of Jerusalem
> I have seen a more shocking thing:
> they commit adultery and walk in lies;
> they strengthen the hands of evildoers,
> so that no one turns from wickedness;
> all of them have become like Sodom to me,
> and its inhabitants like Gomorrah."
> — Jeremiah 23:14

For our first passage in Jeremiah, the sin of Sodom and Gomorrah are compared to the "prophets of Jerusalem" committing adultery and walking in lies. Since adultery is a common image for Israel turning away from God to worship idols, we could speculate that this sin is primarily about turning away from following God. However, even a literal reading that takes this as referring to sexual sins has nothing to do with homosexuality, but with general adultery. In addition, we see deceit and aiding the wicked in their schemes as further reasons for judgement.

The second mention in Jeremiah (49:18), is in reference to the nation of Edom (descendants of Esau). They are being judged for *"The terror you inspire and the pride of your heart"*.

The final mention of Sodom in Jeremiah 50:40 is in reference to Babylon. They are condemned for their idols (50:2, 38, 51:47, 52), their destruction of others (50:15, 29, 51:49), arrogance (50:29, 31-32), and oppression (50:33). Again, there is no mention of homosexuality.

The fourth Lamentation, for Jerusalem

> "...for the wickedness of the daughter of my people
> exceeded the sins of Sodom."
> — LAMENTATIONS 4:6 (NEW JERUSALEM BIBLE)

In Lamentations we see the children of Zion suffering, and dying of starvation (likely a picture of a siege of Jerusalem), for *"the sins of her prophets and the iniquities of her priests, who shed the blood of the righteous in the midst of her"* (LAMENTATIONS 4:6, 13). I chose the reading quality of the New Jerusalem translation over the NRSV for these verses.

Ezekiel accuses Israel of exceeding the sins of Sodom

> "As I live,
> says the Lord God,
> your sister Sodom and her daughters
> have not done as you and your daughters have done.

THE TALE OF SODOM AND GOMORRAH

> This was the guilt of your sister Sodom:
>> she and her daughters had pride,
>> excess of food,
>> and prosperous ease,
> but did not aid the poor and needy.
>
> They were haughty, and did abominable things before me;
>> therefore I removed them when I saw it."
>
> — Ezekiel 16:48-50

The prophet Ezekiel, in a series of verses (16:46-56), has the clearest reference to the sins of Sodom that were being judged. According to this writing, Sodom was judged, not for sexual offenses, but for pride. For having wealth and ease, but refusing to help the poor and needy. We'll be looking more deeply at the phrase "abominable things" in the next chapter covering Leviticus 18. Ezekiel goes on to emphasize that Israel had built upon these sins and become even worse.

While we're looking at this passage in Ezekiel, take note of the promise for Sodom and for Samaria that is added in verse 16:53 —that their fortunes would be restored just as Israel's would be. God's judgement appears to be for a time, for correction and discipline, and even the people of Sodom who are held up as the classic examples of sinful behavior will be restored and blessed. The character of God truly is of reconciliation and redemption.

Amos: overthrowing the wealthy for their oppression of the poor

> "Hear this word, you cows of Bashan
>> who are on Mount Samaria,
>> who oppress the poor, who crush the needy,
>> who say to their husbands, "Bring something to drink!"

"I overthrew some of you,
>   as when God overthrew Sodom and Gomorrah,
>   and you were like a brand snatched from the fire;
>   yet you did not return to me,
> says the Lord."
> — Amos 4:1, 11

The prophet Amos doesn't make as strong a connection to the sins of Sodom and Gomorrah. However, the overthrow of the cities is used as a parallel for the punishment the Lord gave out for the elite wives of the wealthy in Israel who dine lavishly on the backs of the poor.

Zephaniah condemns Moab and the Ammonites

> "Moab shall become like Sodom
>   and the Ammonites like Gomorrah,
>   a land possessed by nettles and salt pits,
>   and a waste forever.
> The remnant of my people shall plunder them,
>   and the survivors of my nation shall possess them.
> This shall be their lot in return for their pride,
>   because they scoffed and boasted
>   against the people of the Lord of hosts."
> — Zephaniah 2:9-10

The final reference in the Tanakh is found in Zephaniah, where the destruction of Moab and the Ammonites (who are descendants of the daughters of Lot—the ones offered to the mob in Sodom) is compared to Sodom and Gomorrah. Their sins are listed as pride and as taunting the nation of Israel (maybe mocking them in their exile and denigrating God's protection?).

We now move to the New Testament, starting with the words of Jesus.

Jesus makes several comparisons

> "If anyone will not welcome you or listen to your words, shake off the dust from your feet as you leave that house or town.
>
> Truly I tell you, it will be more tolerable for the land of Sodom and Gomorrah on the day of judgment than for that town.
> — Matthew 10:14-15

In our first reference (Matthew 10, Luke 10, and in some translations of Mark 6:11) Jesus is sending out the Twelve to proclaim the good news that "the reign of the Heavens has come to you", to heal the sick, and cast out demons. He gives detailed instructions about taking nothing for the journey, finding a worthy host in each village, and staying with this person for the whole visit.

However, he tells them also to expect some lack of welcome as they travel. He compares this lack of hospitality to the sins of Sodom and Gomorrah, even stating that the final state of these cities will be better than the state of these inhospitable towns. Jesus used these stories as examples of the sin of inhospitality to strangers, not of homosexual desire.

In the next comparison Jesus makes (in Matthew 11, similar in Luke 10), we hear that the towns that refused to repent after seeing his miracles are warned of worse outcomes than Sodom.

Finally, we see one more reference from Christ to the events in Sodom in the Gospel of Luke:

> "...but on the day that Lot left Sodom, it rained fire and sulfur from heaven and destroyed all of them — it will be like that on the day that the Son of Man is revealed."
> — Luke 17:29-30

This description was given to the disciples when Jesus gave further explanation to them after answering the Pharisees' question about "when is the kingdom coming?" (his response, paraphrased: "you can't see it the way you're looking for it: it's already among you!"). We could infer that this judgement which is promised here for the Day of the Son of Man has something to do with the people not understanding the gospel and rejecting Christ, similar to the references above in Matthew 11 and Luke 10. The description and comparison of Sodom could be seen to have some parallels with the destruction of Jerusalem in 70 CE, which could be seen to follow from the nation of Israel rejecting the non-violent "Way of Jesus" (as the first believers called it) and seeking for a military messiah to fight Rome.

Paul contrasts some Jewish faithful to the total destruction of Sodom

In Romans 9:29, Paul quotes Isaiah 1:9, previously covered, to support his claim that not all of the Jews have been left out of the selection of the "children of promise" for God's special purposes. He contrasts the situation to the utter destruction of Sodom, declaring that some yet remain.

Peter reassures the tempted faithful

Peter addresses those who are under trial from false teachers and bad influences. He insists that their condemnation is already upon them in the same way that Sodom was made an example:

> "...if by turning the cities of Sodom and Gomorrah to ashes he condemned them to extinction and made them an example of what is coming to the ungodly...
> — 2 Peter 2:6

The specific sins linked to Sodom in this verse are general immoral and lawless behavior. There is a long list of various sins ascribed to these false teachers after this verse but they are not directly linked to the example of Sodom as far as I can tell.

Jude warns against "going after different flesh"

> "Likewise, Sodom and Gomorrah and the surrounding cities, which, in the same manner as they, indulged in sexual immorality and pursued unnatural lust, serve as an example by undergoing a punishment of eternal fire."
> — Jude 1:7

Penultimately, we have a brief statement in the book of Jude which is often tied back to the arguments against gay sexual relationships. Unlike every other description of the sins of Sodom, this passage brings up sexual immorality and "*pursuing unnatural lust*". The NRSV translation we're using notes that this phrase can be more literally translated as "*went after strange flesh*". In further search of the underlying meaning, here's how Young's Literal Translation reads:

> "...as Sodom and Gomorrah, and the cities around them, in like manner to these, having given themselves to whoredom, and gone after *other flesh*, have been set before—an example, of fire age-during, justice suffering."
> — Jude 1:7 (YLT)

What is "strange" or "other" flesh? The Greek word translated here is *heteros* (ἕτερος 2087), and means *"other/another (of a pair), or different"* according to Wiktionary. It may look somewhat familiar, as it is one of the two root words we find in the modern term "heterosexual". Whatever this passage is about, it doesn't seem like it could be describing *same*-sex lust.

Most commentators I've read, including very conservative theologians such as John MacArthur, connect this description, in context of the surrounding verses, with the fact that the men of Sodom were trying to rape angels unawares.

There's a traditionally understood parallel in Genesis 6. The *"sons of God"* reference there is often considered, especially in extra-Biblical Jewish tradition, to be describing angels who are mating with human women. The Apocryphal book of Enoch, written during the inter-testamental period between the Tanakh and the coming of Jesus, is a primary source of this tradition. This is followed immediately by the condemnation from God that leads to the flood. And here we have the reverse—men attempting to rape angels, which results in divine judgement as well.

I'm not sure what lesson we should be receiving today from Jude. Certainly he seems troubled about bad teaching and behavior in the church. I wonder if there was some form of cultic angel worship, including sexual practices, which could have been introduced by some members in the first century after Jesus? After all, the author of Hebrews also spends a good deal of time on the subject of angels as well, making it clear that Christ is over all, is not an angel, and we are not to consider angels as higher than ourselves either. I doubt we'll ever know that one for certain, but it is interesting to consider.

Revelation has the last word

> "...and their dead bodies will lie in the street of the great city that is prophetically called Sodom and Egypt, where also their Lord was crucified."
> — REVELATION 11:9

In Revelation, John refers to Jerusalem as "symbolically" Sodom and Egypt—places that seem to stand for those who reject God's messengers just as it happens in this passage. The two witnesses are killed with the support of many people, before being raised by God.

Summary of references back to the city of Sodom

We've now looked at all the direct references to the city of Sodom throughout the Bible. It is clear that the story of Sodom and Gomorrah is a common reference point for a sinful culture and the fate that awaits similar groups. However, the specific offenses that are listed do not seem to condemn consensual sexual relations regardless of orientation. Inhospitality is key, as well as pride, greed and oppression, and rejection of God's truth.

We have just one more reflection before wrapping up this first verse study and moving on to Leviticus.

Gender and hospitality in ancient cultures and today

Let's set the gay rape question aside for one moment and see what else we can learn from our study in this section about the culture and world-views of those who lived thousands of years ago, and how some continues today.

How we treat foreigners and strangers matters to God

"You shall not wrong or oppress a resident alien,
>for you were aliens in the land of Egypt.

You shall not abuse any widow or orphan.
>If you do abuse them, when they cry out to me,
>>I will surely heed their cry;
>my wrath will burn, and I will kill you with the sword,
>>and your wives shall become widows
>>and your children orphans."
— Exodus 22:21-24

The identification with the stranger and the oppressed is important to God, and important for us also as God-followers. Israel had a very special reason to pay close attention to the marginalized, the poor, and the alien, because God came for them and cared for them when they were in the same situation in Egypt. We can also see from the prophets that the nation of Israel often forgot this aspect of the heart of God. At times they paid careful attention to purity laws and religious rituals, but were condemned for missing the important part (Micah 6).

As Christians, we claim that God is most clearly seen through Jesus of Nazareth. As John records in the 14th chapter of his gospel, Jesus tells his disciples *"Whoever has seen me has seen the Father...Believe me that I am in the Father and the Father is in me; but if you do not, then believe me because of the works themselves."* He was always on the side of the victims, the marginalized, and the oppressed to the point of joining them in crucifixion.

How are women valued?

A modern Western culture that grew up with foundational myths of medieval chivalry can't quite grasp the mindset that would have a father putting the protection of male guests, total strangers, over his own daughters. Lot uses his daughters to try to protect his guests, suggesting that they be raped instead of the men. The same thing happens with the Levite's host, and then the Levite himself personally forces his own wife to take his place during the gang rape in Gibeah.

Not all ancient cultures treated their women this poorly, and I do not want to imply a conclusive judgement from this small sample. However, it seems clear that the men in many cultures around the world did, and still do, place a lower value on women even if they treated them well on average. In this case, some say that part of the reason the hosts were willing to give up daughters (and the Levite his concubine) was because they believed the women were created to be used passively by men, but that a man who is used passively by other men is "reduced" to the level of a women which is the height of shame. We'll return to this same idea later on in covering the New Testament verses.

Sexual practices used for shaming and domination

Rape has a long history of being used to show power and domination over others, in addition to or separate from purely sexual motives. The rapist often is asserting their control over the victim, and the victim recognizes the implicit message of inequality and violent subordination.[20]

---

[20] See the 1988 study "Motivational factors in nonincarcerated sexually aggressive men" by David Link and Susan Roth for example.

Forced sex can happen in prison, war, criminal acts, dating environments, and even in marriage, when the dominant participant overrides the will of the subordinate, of any sex. In ancient times, males raping males could also be seen as a sign of treating the victim as female, which would be considered a great loss of status in these generally misogynistic and patriarchal societies. This could partially explain why Lot and the host in Gibeah were so willing to give up their daughters (who were "intended for this use") to save the male guests from the ultimate humiliation of being treated as women sexually.

Even more disturbing is to realize that this is not over today. There are many sources that paint a picture of male rape being still used in war and political domination to shame and humiliate the enemy. For a few examples, consider the following articles available online:

- *"Powerful myths silence male victims of rape in war"*, by Katie Nguyen at the Thomson Reuters Foundation, Trust.org (2014)
- *"From the DRC to Bosnia, the raping of men is being used as a weapon to destroy 'enemies' and weaken opposition, with devastating results"*, by Graeme Green at CuriousAnimal.com (2014)
- *"The rape of men: the darkest secret of war"*, by Will Storr at TheGuardian.com (2011)
- *"Inside Story: When man rapes man: Victims daren't report it, the law won't recognize it, the public can't understand it: but gradually the taboos around male rape are breaking down, reports Simon Garfield"*, by Simon Garfield at the Independent.co.uk (1992)

Sodomy as a specific sexual act

Finally, it has been generally recognized that the word "sodomy", whether sourced from this Biblical story accurately or not, is most often popularly understood to refer to a specific sexual act otherwise known as anal intercourse. I won't say much here about that other than to say this is not exclusively a gay practice. Some research shows that approximately 30% of heterosexual partners engage in this behavior, and that it is generally not the most popular form of sex within a gay male relationship (some say the percentage is similar to heterosexuals).

This is simply to point out that the common assumption that "homosexuality" can be identified with one specific kind of sexual act, at one time labeled in connection with the story of Sodom, is not accurate.

Conclusion and summary

It's hard for me to see a direct link between homosexual practice in general and the sins of Sodom and Gomorrah. We can certainly learn a lot about behaviors that are not acceptable to God though—rape, violence to strangers, inhospitality, pride, refusal to listen, worship of idols, and oppression of the poor because of greed.

Of course, there are more passages to come that are more strongly linked today to condemnation of homosexuality. The reasons I believed this one was worth discussing in detail are as follows:

- The terms "*sodomy*" and "*sodomite*" are directly related to the story of Sodom. The NRSV (among other Bible versions) translates a Greek word in 1 Corinthians using this English term because of the traditional understanding that male-with-male sex is the main thing condemned in this story in Genesis. Even before we look at that passage, what if *"sodomy"* in a sexual sense could be understood more generally as *"shaming through sexual violence/rape"* regardless of the genders involved? I think we'd all be happy to continue condemning that kind of behavior!

- These stories also give us a glimpse of how men and women were viewed in ancient cultures. The devaluing of women in favor of men is quite disturbing, and may help us understand some later passages as well.

Let's move on to a passage in the Law that is much more clearly describing and condemning at least a certain form of same-gender sexual activity.

*"You shall not lie with a male as with a woman;
it is an abomination."*
— LEVITICUS 18:22 (NRSV)

~ CHAPTER 4 ~
An Abomination in Leviticus 18:22

Now we move into a section of the Tanakh which gives the Law for the Israelite nation. These commandments and expectations are spread throughout the Torah or "Teaching" (first five books), but we will focus on the book of Leviticus for this discussion. There are two parallel verses in chapters 18 and 20. We'll take them one at a time, starting with Leviticus 18:22.

Once again, we'll get started with some questions. Here are what comes to my mind when reading this verse:

1. How do we apply this verse today, keeping in mind how we treat the old laws in general?
2. Does the historic and textual context of the verse add any helpful information about the intent of this prohibition?
3. What is an *abomination* (הְבָעוֹת – *Toebah* or *Toevah*) and what can we learn from this word?

Handling the Law today

I believe the majority of Christians would agree that we are no longer obligated to follow the entirety of the Mosiac Law. Paul is quite adament on this point. However, there are some commandments we find helpful and which have been brought forward to continue on in the New Testament. The question is, how do we know which ones to keep today? What criteria do we use? This is an important question as we look at the two texts from Leviticus.

Here are some examples of practices most evanglical Christians believe are not applicable to us today, but which were originally part of the Law of Moses (cited from Leviticus unless otherwise stated):

- *Forbidding eating pig, rabbit, shellfish, and more (11:4-7)*
- Forbidding crossbreeding animals (19:19)
- Forbidding sowing mixed crops (19:19)
- Forbidding wearing clothes made with more than one kind of fiber (19:19)
- Forbidding cutting the hair on our temples or trimming the corners of our beards (19:27)
- Forbidding getting tattoos (19:28)
- *Forbidding women wearing any men's clothing, and vice-versa* (DEUTERONOMY 22:5)
- All sacrificial rites and practices (many!)
- All cleanliness code, though we certainly use many of the underlying principles (LEVITICUS CHAPTERS 11-15)

Note that the items in italics above are forbidden as *toebah*.

In contrast, I would love to see some of them brought back that we seem to have forgotten, such as:

- No charging of interest on loans to your countrymen, or taking profit from the poor (25:35-37)
- Leaving some product of our labor behind for the poor (19:9-10)
- Treating foreign residents as if they were equal citizens (19:33-34)
- Ban on selling land permanently—preventing the divide between landowners and serfs (25:23)

There is enormous value in reading the laws as Christians today. We certainly should not throw it all away. However, the question we must have in the back of our minds as we read is: "How do we choose which prohibitions still apply?"

Applying the Law today for all sexual issues?

We have some help from the Apostle Paul and the author of the book of Acts on this issue. During some early church debates, most "followers of the Way" (they weren't called Christians until later) assumed that all of the Mosaic code still applied. It wasn't until Peter and James supported Paul's case during the Counsel of Jerusalem that the restrictions were pulled back to *"abstain only from things polluted by idols and from fornication and from whatever has been strangled and from blood."* (Acts 15:20). Later Paul even dismisses the food restrictions in 1 Corinthians 8 and 10, leaving only the general prohibition against "fornication".

It would seem a clear case then to skip past this question since we are dealing with sex. However, even on this topic we don't accept every assumption in the Law about sex and marriage. For example, here are some sexual codes we do not consider to have lasting authority today:

- Sex during a woman's menstrual period is a sin (LEVITICUS 18:19, 20:18).
- Divorce granted if a husband "*[finds] something objectionable about [his wife]*" (DEUTERONOMY 24:1)
- Forced marriage of a rapist, only if caught in the act, to the victim if she is an unengaged virgin (DEUTERONOMY 22:28-29)
- Levirate marriage (marrying your brother's wife when he dies) is an important moral duty (DEUTERONOMY 25:5-6)
- Assumption of having multiple wives (DEUTERONOMY 21:15-17) and concubines.

Setting these questions aside for now, let's proceed with the assumption that we might need to keep the "lie with a man" prohibition applicable today along with the majority of the sexual and idol worship prohibitions. We'll leave the exact ramifications of that for later.

Now that we've looked at the general context of the Law, let's dig deeper into the particular prohibition we're focusing on.

What is the book and chapter context of this verse?

Our first key verse is found in three-quarters through what appears to be a self-contained chapter in the middle of Leviticus, within a section know as the "Holiness Code". The book of Leviticus in general is focused on religious practices for the nation of Israel, and this latter half moves on from instructions to the priests and cleanliness codes to instructions for the people to be holy ("set apart from the nations").

Chapter 18 begins by declaring that the point of rules contained there are to set apart Israel from the nations around them. In the English translations I've studied the chapter is typically divided into four segments:

1. *Introduction:* leave behind practices from Egypt and Canaan and live in God's practices
2. Instructions against sex with close relations.
3. **Instructions against what appear to be a mixture of mostly sexual things, where we find our verse labeled an "abomination".**
4. *Conclusion:* a reminder to follow these rules so that you will not be cast out from your people or your land.

A closer look at the immediate context

Let's look more closely at part 3. At first glance, the immediately surrounding verses may not seem very helpful in our study, but let's list them out here and take another look:

1. Don't have sex with a menstruating woman.
    2. *Don't have sex with your neighbor / kinsman's wife.*
    3. **Don't give your "offspring" to Molech— profaning the name of God.**
    4. *Don't lie with a man as you do a woman.*
5. Don't you (implying "men" at the time) or any women have sex with animals.

The center verse seems oddly out of place at first glance since it seems to be referring to child sacrifice when the rest are just about sex. Maybe we should look into that further to see if there are any clues here.

As I studied this passage, I started considering a specific kind of literary construction which may be in use, as shown by my formatting of the list. Hebrew writers often use what's called a *chiastic* structure where passages build up to and then recede from the most important point (either verse by verse or for an entire book).

Is it possible that we have a chiastic structure in this passage, and if so what would that mean for our understanding of the verses? Regardless of that particular speculation, is it possible that there is a connection between the five instructions which can make sense of the Molech reference?

Seeds, goats, and idols?

When reading the NRSV, it seems at first that the Molech reference is describing a form of child sacrifice, which definitely is described in some other passages. However, Young's Literal Translation uses the word "*seed*" instead of "*offspring*", so I dug deeper. It turns out that instead of using *ben* which is the typical word for child, this verse uses the Hebrew *zera* (זֶרַע 2233). *Zera* carries meanings of seeds for farming, of descendants—hence translated "*offspring*" in the promise to Abraham—and is also used in Leviticus chapter 15 for *semen* (verses 16, 17, 18, and 32). While we're looking at this word, we also see that the verse above (18:20) about having sex with your neighbor's wife also uses *zera*: "*And unto the wife of thy fellow thou dost not give thy **seed** of copulation, for uncleanness with her.*" (YLT)

Going back through the list again, we start with a prohibition against sex with a woman who is bleeding. Both blood and concepts around fertility were very religiously significant in ancient cultures. Could this possibly be referring to pagan sexual rituals involving menustrating women? Next we have a prohibition against "giving your semen" to a neighbor's wife. Why not simply prohit adultery if that's the only meaning here? The specificity of the instructions makes me wonder if there's a particular cultural practice behind this. Then there is a command against giving your "*seed*" to a pagan deity—"*profaning the name of God*"—followed by not lying with a man as you do a woman. The section ends with an admonition against bestility. We may consider one final connection by cross-referencing Leviticus 17:7 which describes goat idol worshipping through sex: "*so that they may no longer offer their sacrifices for goat-demons, to whom they prostitute themselves.*"

The five-item list we're looking at here appears be exclusively describing sexual practices, with the central verse explicitly linking them to idolatrous rituals as if to say: "do not worship Yahweh using the pagan sexual rituals you see around you". My proposal is that we seriously consider the following question:

> *Is it within the realm of possibility that Leviticus 18:22 is prohibiting forms of idol worship which include male-with-male sexual rituals?*

While I do not suggest that we have a conclusive case in thet affirmative, I think that it is a reasonable and strong possibility which explains the context and surrounding verses as well as or better than the conventional understanding.

In fact, one of the most prominent Bible scholars arguing for the traditional side acknowledges: "I do not doubt that the circles out of which Leviticus 18:22 was produced had in view homosexual cult prostitution, at least partly. Homosexual cult prostitution appears to have been the primary form in which homosexual intercourse was practiced in Israel."[21] While the author continues on to insist that the prohibition must be broader, we can see at least seem some agreement on a connection to idol worship practices.

Let's see if we can learn something further by looking directly at the word *"abomination"* which is added to this verse for some kind of emphasis or clarity. It is retroactively applied to everything in the 18th chapter repeatedly in a summary statement (LEVITICUS 18:24-30), but this one prohibition is specifically called out as if to emphasize something about this verse.

What's so special about an "abomination"?

The Hebrew word *toebah* or *toevah* (הַתּוֹעֵבֹת 8441) is traditionally translated into English with a variation of "abomination", "detestable" or "abhorrent". It is only used in two sections in Leviticus—once in 18:22, four times in the summary of chapter 18, and once in 20:13. However, it appears in the Tanakh 114 times in total (by my count), from Genesis to Malachi.

What does it mean? See Strong's definition here:

> **To-ay-baw'** (toebah) feminine active participle of ta'ab
> (*'make to be abhorred, be, commit more, utterly'*)
> properly, something disgusting (morally),
> i.e. (as noun) an abhorrence;
> especially idolatry or (concretely) an idol
> – abominable (custom, thing), abomination.
> — STRONG'S EXHAUSTIVE CONCORDANCE (1890)

---

21 "The Bible and Homosexual Practice", by Robert Gagnon

The 1906 Brown-Driver-Briggs Hebrew and English Lexicon has the following definition:

Tow`ebah: A disgusting thing, abomination, abominable
– in ritual sense (of unclean food, idols, mixed marriages)
– in ethical sense (of wickedness etc)

It's clear that anything labeled an "abomination" is declared wrong for cultural, religious or ethical reasons at the time. Practices known as *toebah* were certainly off-limits for ancient Israel, directly connected to the idea of being set apart for God from the practices of the nations around them.

However, our definition does not indicate which prohibitions are uniquely lasting for us today. Some of the practices called "abominations" are no longer considered on the same absolute immoral level by most Christians today, whether or not they should be. Here are some examples of other actions declared *toebah* from the Law and the Prophets:

- Eating pig, rabbit and shellfish, among other things—no lobster or shrimp allowed. (LEVITICUS 11:4-7)
- Women wearing men's clothing, and vice-versa (DEUTERONOMY 22:5)[22]
- Not helping the poor and needy when you have resources to do so (EZEKIEL 16:50-58)
- Charging interest on loans and making a profit on the backs of the poor (EZEKIEL 18:5-18, 22:11)

If a conservative argument is made that *toebah* marks practices which are uniquely condemned by God for all time and

---

[22] Some pagan temple rituals involved cross-dressing, e.g. for Aphroditus.

still apply today in contrast to some of the other sections of the law, then we would have to follow this rule with all 114 others to be consistent. Beyond that diffficulty, I would like to point out that the beginning of Leviticus chapter 18 clearly states that the purpose of these rules are to set the nation of Israel apart from those around them at the time.

Looking for "abominations" throughout the Bible

I decided to cross-reference every other use of the Hebrew word in the Bible to get a better sense of use in context, which sometimes takes reading several chapters around the exact verse. After over eight hours of study, tagging each verse with one or more general categories, here's what I found:[23]

- The primary use of the word refers to false or idol worship (60%). Greed, injustice, and other moral failures cover another quarter of usage, leaving only 15% to refer to sexual immorality and prostitution.
- Even having counted each repetition of the word in the Leviticus 18 summary separately in this category, only 7 usages have anything to do with same-sex acts. Excluding this repetition, we have only two unique verses explicitly connecting some form of same-sex relations with *toebah*.
- In the Pentateuch alone, 19 of 25 unique usages explicitly prohibit some form of false worship.
- In Genesis the word is used to describe *Egyptian prejudices*—against eating with the Hebrews, shepherds in general, and making sacrifices to Yahweh.

---

23 Compiled into spreadsheet: http://bit.ly/HS-toebah

The word seems to be used in one of the following ways (listed generally by frequency of use):

1. Idols and idol worship specifically.
2. False worship of all kinds, especially child sacrifice (to Molech, often in the valley of Gehenna).
3. Oppression and injustice, seen as rooted in greed.
4. Certain sexual practices often related to prostitution.
5. Cultural taboos of the time (Egyptian prejudices, food and clothing laws).

At the risk of oversimplification, I believe a simple verse lookup like this shows a very strong connection of *toebah* to practices associated with pagan idol worship and prostitution. And the references to Egypt's disgust toward Hebrew practices means that we cannot deny it can be used in a culturally relevent way that does not set a universal unchanging standard.

You can find all the verses cross-referenced online, and we won't take the time to go through all of them here. I would like to look at just one section of passages before we conclude.

Similar lists in Ezekiel

During the study I found a couple of passages in Ezekiel chapters 18 and 22 when doing my research that might help us think about this. They list a variety of *toebah* which contain two of the five prohibitions found in Leviticus 18:19-23—having sex with the neighbor's wife, and with menstruating women. Theses are associated with further prohibitions on idol worship and a variety of oppressions and injustices, yet there is no explicit mention of "male-with-male" relations.

Support for "abomination" linked to sexual worship practices

There is one final set of connections worth pointing out as we look at the minority of *toebah* clearly associated with sexuality:

- "male cult prostitution" (1 Kings 14:24)
- paying for Yahweh sacrifices with wages from cult prostitution (Deuteronomy 23:18)
- prostitutes on the "high places" (Ezekiel 16)
- the "harlot" or "adultery" imagery applied to Israel's false worship (Ezekiel 6:9, 23:36)
- all the references including mentions of idols (45 times) and sacrificing to Molech (17 times)

Once we start compile all these references there seems to be some reasonable support for a reading of Leviticus 18:19-23 as a list of idolatrous practices instead of a list of general sexual prohibitions. Sexual prohibitions associated with *toebah* seem to be connected to pagan worship practices pretty consistently.

We'll cover some of this again as we move on to the next chapter, referencing another verse with a lot of parallels.

Summary of looking at Leviticus 18:22

So, what did we cover here?

1. As Christians, we don't consider Mosaic Law directly authoritative to our faith, but we find much value there—provided we know how to apply it forward properly.
2. In context, the prohibition against male-with-male sex could be referring specifically to pagan sexual worship practices that were in active use in surrounding nations.

3. The attachment of the word *toevah* ("abomination") to a prohibition has no extra, unique lasting significance for us today, but it is fairly often linked to idolatrous worship practices.

My personal conclusion after studying this verse in-depth and in context is that there is enough evidence for a connection to pagan cult worship rituals *to make it hard to be sure* that this is a general statement against all same-sex intimate relationships of any kind, for all time.

Even if this prohibition is broader than specifically applying to pagan worship practices, one could argue that it may still not apply to today's environment because it had to do with the ancient Israelites setting themselves apart from other tribes. Since the surrounding nations often associated same-sex relations with idol worship, Israel was told to avoid it as a cultural taboo of the period, similar to the food and clothing rules. Our culture no longer understands same-sex relationships to be idol worship practices, so we would not have the same problem.

> *If a man lies with a male as with a woman,*
> *both of them have committed an abomination;*
>
> *they shall be put to death;*
> *their blood is upon them."*
> — Leviticus 20:13

CHAPTER 5
The Death Penalty in Leviticus 20

Jumping forward two chapters from our previous reference, we find the *"male lying with male"* prohibition repeated, but this time with a specific punishment attached. And it's quite straightforward: *"they shall be put to death"*. What do we do with this?

Once again, I start with a few questions:

1. What is the context for this verse, and why is the prohibition repeated so soon after the first reference?
2. What are the general parameters for calling for the death penalty in Scripture?
3. What can we learn by from the assignment of the death penalty to this prohibition?

The context in Leviticus 20

As a reminder, we're in a section of Leviticus referred to as the Holiness Code which started in chapter 17. Similar to the rest of the book, it is divided into multiple sections which mostly line up with our traditional chapter divisions. Each section begins with a variation of the phrase:

> "The Lord spoke to Moses, saying..."
> — LEVITICUS 20:1 (PATTERN)

So there is a sense where each is somewhat of a self-contained section, yet all very much connected into the larger theme of holiness, or being set apart. Some sections seem to have a stronger focus than others. For example, chapter 17 is mostly about blood, death and sacrifices, chapter 19 seems more eclectic, covering idols, sacrifices, the poor, justice, farming, and much more, and chapter 21 is focused on holiness for those practicing as priests.

The theme in the self-contained 20th chapter of Leviticus, as I read it, seems to be about prescribing the appropriate penalties for transgressions which have already been prohibited elsewhere in the book. The punishments outlined in this section are primarily a form of capital punishment, followed by some kind of banishment or outlawing from the people. Here's the list:

1. **Death** (*stoning*): Giving children to Molech. Stoned and cut off from the people.
2. **Banishment:** Following magicians or spirits of the dead.
3. **Death:** Cursing your mother or father.

4. **Death:** A man committing adultery with his neighbor's wife, both executed.
5. **Death:** Man having sex with his father's wife, both executed.
6. **Death:** Man having sex with his daughter-in-law, both executed.
7. **Death:** Man having sex with another man, both executed.
8. **Death** (*burned alive*): Man marrying a woman and her mother, all executed.
9. **Death:** Man or woman having sex with an animal, kill both person and animal.
10. **Death** (*public execution*): Man having sex with a sister or half-sister, both executed.
11. **Banishment:** Man having sex with a menstruating woman, both outlawed.
12. **"Bearing Consequences"**: Sex with aunt—"they will bear the consequences of their guilt", unspecified.
13. **Die Childless:** Man marrying his brother's wife (presumably while the brother is living, because otherwise he's commanded to marry her in Levirate Law).

Before we get deeper into the topic, note that both men and women are singled out for bestiality, but only men are the focus of same-gender sex in both of the Old Testament references. The only mention of women engaging in same-gender sex in the entire Bible is one verse in the Epistle to the Romans.

The chapter ends with a repeat of the exhortation to keep the laws, putting them into practice, so that *"the land to which I bring you to settle in may not vomit you out"* (LEVITICUS 20:22). They are to be consecrated to Yahweh—set apart from the other peoples.

After chapter 20 ends, the text moves away from assigning punishments into stipulating further rules. That's the textual context as far as I can make out.

Since the focus seems to be on the death penalty, let's look at that subject more closely.

Capital punishment in the Tanakh

Leviticus chapter 20 clearly has a focus on prescribing death for various offenses. However, it's not the only place where this final form of punishment is commanded.

Other capital offenses in the Law

Here's a short list of some other actions throughout the Tanakh which are assigned the death penalty:

- New brides who can't prove their virginity are stoned to death at her father's house. If the accusing husband is proven wrong, he is fined. (DEUTERONOMY 22:20-21)
- A rapist must be executed—but also his victim if they are in the city and no one hears her. (DEUTERONOMY 22:23-27)
- The daughter of a priest who becomes a prostitute must be burned alive. (LEVITICUS 21:9)
- God promises the sword against abusers of orphans and widows. (EXODUS 22:22-24)
- Someone who speaks God's name in a curse must be stoned by the community. (LEVITICUS 24:14-16, 23)
- Going up on, or even touching, Mount Sinai when Moses was on it. (EXODUS 19:12)

- Not respecting the Sabbath rest. (Exodus 31:14, carried out in Numbers 15:32-36)
- Preaching a different god—up to killing an entire city if drawn away. (Deuteronomy 13)
- Any "outsider" (a non-Levite?) who comes near the tabernacle during set up or tear down. (Numbers 1:51)
- A son who does not obey his parents should be stoned. (Deuteronomy 21:18-21)
- Most murders, but with some exemptions if killing a slave. (Exodus 21:20-21)
- Kidnapping with intent to sell people into slavery. (Exodus 21:16)
- Anyone who does not accept the decision of a judge or priest. (Deuteronomy 18:8-13)
- The keeper of a bull that kills after being known as dangerous. (Exodus 21:29)
- Robbers, idolaters, murderers, adulterers, those who oppress the poor and needy, and those who take interest on loans or keep collateral are condemned in Ezekiel 18.

By the count I have, 36 of the 613 commandments in the Tanakh are given the death penalty.

What would this punishment look like?

Most references to capital punishment in the Tanakh are simply described as being *"put to death"* with no methods prescribed. Stoning and burning alive are specifically designated for a few cases.

To aid us in understanding how these rules were interpreted and applied by the nation of Israel, we can read ancient oral commentaries known as *Mishnah* which were gradually compiled into a written collection called the *Talmud* after the destruction of the temple in 70 CE. These contain a variety of viewpoints on Scripture, functioning as commentaries for teaching and debate. Jesus would likely have been familiar with many of these teachings as oral tradition. From these resources, we can learn more about what execution might have looked like.

Here are descriptions of the four traditional methods of capital punishment as understood from the Tanakh:

1. **Stoning** (*sekila*)
    a. "This was performed by pushing a person off a height of at least 2 stories. If the person didn't die, then the executioners (the witnesses) brought a rock that was so large that it took both of them to lift it; this was placed on the condemned person to crush them."
    b. "...the other view says that it was carried out much as one thinks and, as seems to be specified in *Shoftim* (17:7), the first stones are thrown by the two witnesses."
2. **Burning** (*serefah*)
    "This was done by melting lead, and pouring it down the throat of the condemned person."
3. **Decapitation** (*hereg*)
    Also known as "*being put to the sword*" or *beheading*.
4. **Strangulation** (*chenek*)
    a. "A rope was wound around the condemned person's neck, and the executioners (the witnesses) pulled from either side to strangle the condemned person."

b. "It was accomplished by having the convict stand in mud up to his or her knees, after which a pair of scarves were wound around the neck and then pulled in opposite directions by two witnesses."

Examining stoning, or "lapidation", as a form of execution

The classic understanding of stoning describes an execution in which the condemned is brought out into a public space and the community gathers around taking turns at throwing rocks until death ensues. The rules often specify the dimensions of stones used, making sure that they are neither too small nor too large. This ensures that death does not come too quickly. The intent in stoning is that there is a period of extreme suffering before death, similar to the Roman method of crucifixion.

Stoning has a long history, being mentioned in ancient Greek texts as well as in the Torah and the Talmud. While it is not mentioned in the Qur'an itself, and scholars debate if the practice is consistent with Islam, the collection of reports on the life and actions of Muhammad called the Hadith do describe stoning.

Modern forms still on the books or used extrajudicially in some Middle-Eastern and African countries require the condemned to be restrained through partially burying their body so they can attempt to escape over the 15-20 minutes it takes for them to be beated to a bloody stump. It is death through torture.

> Stoning is a cruel form of torture that is used to punish men and women for adultery and other 'improper' sexual relations. It is currently sanctioned by law and carried out by state actors in at least two countries, and at least seven individuals have been stoned to death in the last five years.

— Terman and Fijaki, *Stoning is Not Our Culture*[24]

This is apparently the form of stoning that the first Christian martyr, Stephen, suffered in Acts chapter 7. The apostle Paul, then an approving bystander, also undergoes but survives a stoning later in his life as recorded in Acts chapter 14.

According to Judaic tradition, stoning was the execution method of choice for violation of Leviticus 20:13. It's likely that the classic picture of stoning that we get from the New Testament was more of a mob killing scenario than a judicial ruling—especially since the Jews had no authority to execute under the Romans. So we're probably looking at the "push off the rooftop and be crushed by a boulder" scenario here. Regardless, this is not a pleasant death. Decapitation was the only method which minimized suffering during execution, yet the Law required other forms for violations like this one.

What do we do with all this?

When we seek to understand and apply this ancient, inspired, sacred text to our lives today, it's vitally important that we are consistent and conscientious in our study and reflection. It's not fair to apply one rule strictly while letting others slide, or to ignore the seriousness of thecommands we have here.

There are two big questions that I believe we must engage with as Christians living in the 20th century today:

1. If we're going to apply the traditional interpretation of this law in our world today, shouldn't we be required to

---

24 Terman, Rochelle and Fijabi, Mufuliat. *Stoning is Not Our Culture: A Comparative Analysis of Human Rights and Religious Discourses in Iran and Nigeria*. The Global Campaign to Stop Killing and Stoning Women. 2010.

execute all men who have sex with men regardless of their faith? By what interpretive method can we insist on the lasting prohibition yet ignore the prescribed consquence, as most conservatives on this issue do?

2. Are we sure that capital punishment for every one of these offenses is God's divinely dictated, absolute, unquestionable **ideal practice for all time**? If not for every one of them, how do we apply this today?

These are tough questions, but they must be asked if we continue to insist on using the Mosaic Law to inform our ethics and religious practices.

For myself, I believe we can affirm the inspired source of these commands in the ancient context they were given, yet also understand God to be on the move, pushing us ever further toward love and mercy instead of exclusion and punishment. I wonder if a literal, unquestioning reading of the Tanakh as static rules applicable to all times and cultures has too often led to things that the majority of Christians would find inconsistent with Jesus's teachings, and if God is wanting us to ask some bigger questions.

Modern Judaism on capital punishment

In my research, it seems that we Christians aren't the only ones who were bothered by these punishments. At least by around the time of Jesus, tradition had affirmed the justice of these executions in theory, but made them almost impossible to apply in practice. The list of requirements for a crime to be assigned the death penalty reads almost like a Marx Brothers comedy avoidance routine:

- Two witnesses must have observed the crime (if they are proven lying, they are executed instead). They must be:
  - Adult Jewish professional men who keep the commandments and know both written and oral law;
  - Must see each other at the time of the sin;
  - Have no speech or hearing problem (for warning);
  - Cannot not be related to each other or the accused.
- Both of them had to give a warning (*hatra'ah*) to the person that they are about to commit a capital offense;
- Must warn the criminal only seconds before the crime;
- In those same few seconds, the person about to sin must:
  - Respond that s/he was familiar with the punishment, but they were going to sin anyway;
  - Begin to commit the sin/crime;
- The court had to examine each witness separately; and if even one minor detail of their evidence was contradictory, like eye color, the entire evidence was thrown out;
- The court had to consist of minimally 23 judges;
- The majority could not be a simple majority—the split verdict that would allow conviction had to be at least 13 to 11 in favor of conviction;
- Any unanimous verdict of guilty was thrown out, because if no judge could find anything exculpatory about the accused, there must be something wrong with the court.
- Witnesses must also serve as the executioners.[25]

Jesus addresses the application of the Law in Matthew 15 (and Mark 7). He calls the Pharisees and scribes hypocrites for avoiding prominent laws like the death penalty for those

---

25 https://en.wikipedia.org/wiki/Capital_and_corporal_punishment_in_Judaism

who do not honor their parents, and yet forcing others to obey minor rules such as hand-washing which they had accused him of breaking.

> Then Pharisees and scribes came to Jesus from Jerusalem and said, "Why do your disciples break the tradition of the elders? For they do not wash their hands before they eat."
>
> He answered them, "And why do you break the commandment of God for the sake of your tradition? For God said, 'Honor your father and your mother,' and, 'Whoever speaks evil of father or mother must surely die.' But you say that whoever tells father or mother, 'Whatever support you might have had from me is given to God,' then that person need not honor the father. So, for the sake of your tradition, you make void the word of God. You hypocrites! Isaiah prophesied rightly about you when he said:
>
>> 'This people honors me with their lips,
>>   but their hearts are far from me;
>> in vain do they worship me,
>>   teaching human precepts as doctrines.' "
>
> — MATTHEW 15:1-4

While I've seen some people try to make the case that Jesus is endorsing capital punishment in this statement, it seems more likely that he has no problem with the execution not being applied. Jesus himself appears to have little regard for the commandment to honor parents both in his own life (MARK 3:31-35) and in teachings to his disciples (LUKE 14:26). His concern appears to be for the hypocrisy of the rule-enforcers, and the principle behind the law from which they were benefiting financially by allowing people to break (allowing for wealth to be set aside for future donation to the temple so they were "unable" to care for their needy parents but could enjoy it in the meantime).

The story of Jesus and the woman caught in adultery in John chapter 8 shows his attitude toward applying the death penalty prescribed in the Law. By a strict interpretation of the Law, he should have told the Pharisees to stone her. Yet, here he applies his new interpretation of the Law (*"You have heard that it was said in ancient times [referring directly to the Law]...but I say to you..."*) with a heart for the person, not the commandment.

Jewish scholars today, even the strictly literal Orthodox, generally hold to the interpretation that the commandments with death penalties are for emphasis, not for practice.

> "R. Eliezer b. Azariah says: A Sanhedrin that effects a capital punishment once in 70 years is branded a destructive tribunal. R. Tarfon and R. Akiva say: Were we members of the Sanhedrin, no person would ever be put to death."
> — Mishnah Makkot 1:10

> "It is better and more satisfactory to acquit a thousand guilty persons than to put a single innocent one to death."
> — 12th-century Jewish legal scholar Maimonides

The only crimes for which you can be executed in theory in the modern state of Israel today are war crimes, genocide (including the Holocaust), and treason. And even then it doesn't really happen much. Though faced with constant terrorist activity, the courts in modern Israel have only ever executed two individuals, both prominent Nazis.

After being confronted with the proliferation of brutal

terrorist acts, the military courts stated that, though the death penalty may be more appropriate, they were bound "to uphold principles of the State of Israel, the moral concepts of Jewish tradition, in which a Sanhedrin that passed a death sentence was considered to be 'a bloody Sanhedrin.'"

— Professor Menachem Elon

Applying the death penalty in Leviticus

We could go much further in the discussion of the death penalty, but will leave that for another conversation. What is important to remember for this topic is to remember that a literal reading and application of Leviticus 20 as interpreted by tradition would require us to execute all gay males who have ever engaged in sex. Fortunately there are very few American evangelical Christians who advocate for this.[26]

Using the death penalty to cross-reference commandments

Leaving the death penalty debate behind, we can further explore our main topic by cross-referencing other prohibitions in Scripture which call for capital punishment. These crimes are a minority across all of the Law. Judaic tradition holds that there are 613 different commandments total, but only 36 them call for execution if violated. Because it is a small group, and many of the rules are repeated across multiple books (primarily Exodus, Leviticus and Deuteronomy), we can make some comparisons

---

[26] Pastors such as Steven L. Anderson, Kevin Swanson, Phillip Kayser and members of the Westboro Baptist Church do call for the death penalty.

between each collection of laws.

Every one of the prohibitions connected to the death penalty in Leviticus is repeated in the book of Deuteronomy, with just one exception. The command against male-with-male sex that we have been looking at is not to be found. However, there is an added prohibition in Deuteronomy against *"male cult prostitutes"* or *"qadesh"* (שָׁדֵק 6945) which were otherwise not mentioned by name in Leviticus. Continuing from our previous conclusion that Leviticus 18 could be describing an idol worship practice, we could see this new mention as a parallel prohibition further clarifying the banned practice as a religious ritual rather than a condemnation of gay partnership.

Ancient pagan worship practices often involved sexual acts at temples and shrines. Both male and female prostitutes were available for fertility rites with male worshipers. We can find these practices mentioned in a few other places in Scripture.

Judah and Tamar

In Genesis 38 we find Judah purchasing the services of someone he believes to be a *"wayside prostitute"* (turns out to be his daughter-in-law Tamar—we'll get to that in a minute) while on a journey. When he attempts to send the payment later, he enters the nearby town and openly asks the people *"where is the temple prostitute who was [here]?"* (GENESIS 38:21).

The Hebrew word used here is *qedeshah* (הַשְּׁדֵקָה 6948), which is the feminine version of *qadesh* (שָׁדֵק 6945). Both are directly related to the concept of consecrating or devoting something to sacred duty, *qadash* (שָׁדַק 6942), as used to describe some of the following things in the Tanakh:

- the Sabbath (GENESIS 2:3)
- the people of God (EXODUS 19:10)
- the tabernacle (EXODUS 29:44)
- the priests (EXODUS 28:3)

In the story about Judah, he's referring to prostitutes who are consecrated for sacred duty in sexual worship rituals. This concept was translated by the King James scholars as *"sodomite"* or *"unclean"* after the pattern of the Greek Septuagint translation which Jesus would have been familiar with. However, that is a misleading interpretation because the literal meaning is clearly associated with worship rather than the city of Sodom or the group rape and violence it was known for in general:

> **Qadesh:** Male temple prostitute.
> From qadash; a *"sacred/set-apart person,"*
> a devotee (by prostitution) to licentious idolatry
> — STRONG'S EXHAUSTIVE CONCORDANCE

Finally, when it is reported that Tamar is pregnant, Judah orders her to be *burned alive*. It's only when she reveals how she tricked Judah into carrying out the duties he was required to perform by Levirate marriage rules that she is allowed to live. As we've seen, this execution method was prescribed later in the law for the daughters of priests who enter into prostitution—maybe because they were getting involved in sacred cult prostitution?

Male temple prostitutes in Israel

The *qadesh* do not disappear in the nation of Israel after the law is given. The practice of prostitutes used in pagan temple worship rituals continues along with all the other Canaanite idol worship throughout the nation's existence:

> For they also built for themselves high places, pillars, and sacred poles on every high hill and under every green tree; there were also **male temple prostitutes** *[qadesh]* in the land. They committed all the abominations *[idolatry?]* of the nations that the Lord drove out before the people of Israel.
> — KINGS 14:23-24

The term is repeated in three more passages in Kings describing how various rulers attempted to clear the land of idol worship practices by expelling the *qadesh* and destroying their houses (1 KINGS 15:12; 22:46, 2 KINGS 23:7). Hosea describes the men of Israel going to *"sacrifice with temple prostitutes [qadesh]"* (HOSEA 4:14, also 6:10). Job discusses how the life of the godless *"ends among the temple prostitutes [qadesh]"* (JOB 36:14, NRSV NOTE).

It's clear that cult worship of idols using male prostitution was a constant religious concern for the faithful Israelites in these centuries. Now that there are reasonable ways to connect both verses in Leviticus to this regularly condemned practice, we might want to be more cautious about insisting that God was divinely prohibiting the possibility of monogamous, intimate relationships for all time for those he has created in this unique way.

Summary of looking at Leviticus 20:13

While the text of the prohibition itself did not change from the previous chapter, I hope we've been able to gain some insight based on the punishment that was assigned only in the current verse. Here's what I hope you're leaving this chapter with:

1. If we are going to literally apply Leviticus' prohibition against *"man lying with a male"* to all homosexual relationships today, we must take the associated death penalty seriously.
2. By cross-referencing the book of Deuteronomy on all actions worthy of the death penalty, there may be a connection to the much more specific prohibition against *"male cult prostitution"*.
3. Notice that concerns about male temple prostitutes are more commonly mentioned in Scripture than anything about homosexuality in general. Keep this in mind as we continue on to the New Testament.

Next, we move into the New Testament age by looking at some of Saint Paul's writings.

*...the law is laid down not for the innocent but
for the lawless and disobedient,
for the godless and sinful,
for the unholy and profane,
for those who kill their father or mother,
for murderers, fornicators, sodomites,
slave traders, liars, perjurers,
and whatever else is contrary to the sound teaching...*
— 1 Timothy 1:9b-10a

— CHAPTER 6 —
What are the Arsenokoites in 1 Timothy?

There are only three verses traditionally cited as directly prohibiting same-sex relationships in the New Testament. While principles on many issues can be draw from broader sources, we will focus on these specific selections. We begin our first New Testament study in the letter of 1 Timothy.

Our first two out of the three passages both use the Greek word *arsenokoites*, translated "*sodomites*" in the NRSV above. I decided to look at this verse before the parallel in 1 Corinthians because a second word we should look at is added there. We will build on this word study in the following chapter.

Here are my questions for our discussion of 1 Timothy:

1. Is there anything different about our study of the New Testament, compared to the Tanakh?
2. What is this *arsenokoites* word? What does it mean?
3. What is the author's[27] teaching intent in this passage?

Studying in the New Testament

Now that we're moving into the New Testament, there are a few differences we'll find in our study methods. I'll try to explain how and why I'm approaching things in this section.

Cross-referencing in the canon is not possible

We've spent a lot of time in cross-referencing word studies for our first three passages in the Tanakh. I hope you'll agree that it was helpful to pull together a variety of references for each passage to help us get at the meaning of the instructions.

Unfortunately this is more difficult for the next verses. There are no other places in Scripture where the same words are used, or other sections that refer back to them. We are left with three brief verses which seem to stand alone. What we can do is:

1. Realize that these passages are written with deep knowledge and reverence for the Tanakh.
2. Cross-reference Greek and Roman texts of the era for both language and cultural cues.

---

[27] While some Bible scholars believe that 1 Timothy was written later by an anonymous disciple of Paul in his name posthumously (an accepted practice at the time), we'll use the traditional attribution of Paul for this chapter.

3. And read the verses in their broader contexts to understand how they contribute to the overall message.

A brief summary of what we've learned in the Tanakh

After our examination in the last few chapters, I believe it's clear that the Tanakh witness against all homosexual relationships is not as unambiguous as the straight reading of a modern English translation might have us think. At minimum, we can agree that Scripture contains stories and laws strongly opposing:

1. Violent inhospitality toward "outsiders", including examples of both same-sex and opposite-sex rape.
2. "Abominable" practices which violate cultural and/or ethical norms, including at least some form(s) of male-with-male sex.
3. Participation in ritual cult prostitution, particularly with males and daughters of priests.

While women are prohibited from engaging in sexual activity with animals (bestiality), there are no rules against being in a lesbian relationship in the Tanakh. It is only *prostitution in idolatrous rituals* which are a concern for both genders.

While the concern about idolatrous rituals could be carried forward to our third New Testament passage, what we encounter in the first two passages may come from exposure to a whole new world of vice and immorality.

Changing languages and cultural settings

It's important to remember that the Israelites of Paul's day lived in a completely different cultural and linguistic environment from those of earlier times.

As we discussed in our first Leviticus passage, rules of morality often are in response to the surrounding environment. Israel was commanded to be set apart from the practices of Canaanite idolatry and given new codes for living as the people of Yahweh within a tribal Middle-Eastern ~1500 BCE context.

By the time Paul wrote his letters to the early churches, so much had changed for his people, religion and nation:

- The rise and fall of the kings of Israel and Judah (1,000-600 BCE).
- The exile and assimilation of the Ten Lost Tribes by Assyria (750 BCE).
- Exile of Judah under Babylon (586-538 BCE).
- The exiles return under Persian rule (538-333 BCE).
- Alexander the Great conquers Persia and the Greeks rule Israel (333-160 BCE).
- When Antiochus IV Epiphanes tries to replace Judaism with Greek religion, the Maccabees successfully revolt and priest-kings rule for a time (160-63 BCE).
- General Pompey besieges Jerusalem, and Judea becomes a Roman kingdom (63 BCE).
- Judea is converted to a Roman province in 6 CE.

From the 3rd century BCE on, a massive cultural exchange with Greece was started. The Jews began to be exposed to Greek culture, philosophy and religion, while also translating the Tanakh from Hebrew and Aramaic into Greek. During this period the Greek translation known as the Septuagint became a primary source for many, and additional writings which we now know as the Apocrypha were added. Judaism expanded outward dramatically, establishing synagogues in far off regions and developing significant new centers of learning and study in locations such as Alexandria in Egypt.

By the time of Christ, Aramaic was the common language spoken locally in Judea, but Greek was the international trade language. Not only was Paul writing in Greek, with which he would have grown up as a Hellenized Jew and Roman citizen, but he was writing to those who were very familiar with Greek and Roman culture whether they were ethnically Jewish or Gentile. The cultural assumptions and environments were vastly different from those in Genesis and Leviticus.

Greco-Roman Sexuality, and Pederasty

Men's roles were to be heads of house-holds (for the wealthy this could include wife, children and slaves). Wives were the source of progeny, but there was broad acceptance for and sometimes even a foundational assumption that sexual pleasure for men was to be sought outside the family. This could include either opposite-sex or same-sex liasons.

It's clear from many Greco-Roman authors that certain forms of same-sex relationships were accepted and encouraged by many, though not by all. The most idealized form was known as *paiderastia*, from which we derive the word "pederasty", which dates back to the 7th century BCE. This was a very specific relationship between an older man (the "lover", *erastês*) and a young man (the "beloved", *erômenos*) 13-20 years of age. In theory it could be a purely platonic relationship between a mentor and someone seeking wisdom, but it often included sex too.

There were several unique characteristics which make this relationship very different from that of most modern same-sex couples:

1. **Not exclusively homosexual:** The lover was usually married to a woman at the same time. The marriage bond was for property and progeny, and pleasure was assumed to be sought elsewhere (whether from men or women). It wasn't until the 20th century that marriage was seen to be about complete sexual fulfillment.
2. **Inequality:** The sexual relationship was completely one-sided in favor of the lover. The beloved was not expected to have pleasure or a voice in the relationship.
3. **Impermanence:** The beloved was usually rejected and replaced by a younger male after outgrowing their youth. The new adult may then have their own beloved.
4. **Humiliation:** There was always great potential for humiliation and abuse in this relationship, which was generally under the control of the lover. Both Plutarch and Plato discuss the potential for abuse toward the beloved, and the beloved's hatred in return.
5. **Male-dominated:** There is some evidence of ancient Greek lesbian love affairs, most famously from the poet Sappho from the Isle of Lesbos, but the men doing most of the recording during this period didn't give it much time or respect. It was not an accepted cultural practice in the way that male relationships were.

Being perceived as a passive partner in a relationship between those of similar ages was predominately seen as humiliating and inappropriate for adult men because they would be associated with the culturally "inferior" women. It was socially acceptable for men to take this role only as a youth, and then find their own *erômenos* as they became an adult. There were some famous partners who broke these rules, but it was not the normal behavior and at least one of the men would risk losing his reputation.

There were at least two other forms of same-sex arrangements recorded in Greco-Roman culture.

The second option was for men to seek sex with male youth either in brothels or in their own households as slaves. In these cases there was quite clearly no choice for the slave boy (at least the *erômenos* had a choice to begin with). Some men were so taken with these boys that they would be castrated to preserve their more feminine appearance longer. The emperor Nero is famous for doing so with a slave named Sporus around this time period, and then marrying him in an elaborate ceremony.

This owner/slave relationship is decidedly one-sided and not comparable to a reciprocal relationship between two equal partners. I think we would all agree it is not something we'd ever want to support.

I'll leave the third (and most despised even by the Greeks and Romans) form of same-sex relationships for our discussion of 1 Corinthians since it may be more directly encountered there.

The Epistles as unique literature

Finally, we should not forget that we are now looking at a completely new form of literature compared to the rest of the canon. Unlike the various histories, poetry, laws, and narratives, Paul is writing letters.

These letters were written for specific reasons to specific audiences, at a specific period. While there is disagreement amongst Biblical scholars as to the date (between 60 and 150 CE) and therefore the exact author and recipient of this particular letter, we know that it is generally written to a community in Ephesus that was started by Paul and led by Timothy.

The most important thing to know for our current study is that the letter was originally intended for those living in the middle of Greco-Roman culture, and that they would understand various references and terms from their context in ways that we wouldn't today.

Finally we get to that long Greek word: ἀρσενοκοίτης

Now that we've established some background for our New Testament study, let's dig into the text by examining the Greek word *arsenokoites*. This time we have some real digging to do.

The Apostle Paul makes up words

Paul may or may not have been the first to use the word in speech, but he appears to be the first to write it down. It's only found in twice in the Bible, both times in a list of various immoral behaviors. There are very few recorded uses of *arsenokoites* after his time as well. Most of the other usages are from Christian texts which simply quote Paul's writings, which makes it very difficult to have confidence in our definition of it today.

Before we discuss the likely origin, I would like to emphasize that much of the conservative doctrine against homosexuality is based directly on this single word on which contemporary scholars, both liberal and conservative, agree *we can never be absolutely sure* what it meant when Paul wrote it down.

The most common conservative argument for the derivation of the word is the hypothesis that Paul created it based on the early Greek translation from Hebrew of Leviticus 18:22 found in the Septuagint:

καὶ μετὰ *ἄρσενος* οὐ κοιμηθήσῃ *κοίτην* γυναικός βδέλυγμα γάρ ἐστιν

The suggestion is that it's a compound made up of the Greek words for "male" (ἄρσην 730) and "bed" (κοίτη 2845), as highlighted above. The word for "bed" can be a euphemism for sex, as used by the 3rd century BCE translators of the Septuagint. Some speculate that Paul used this word as a shortened reference to the entire prohibition in Leviticus. This would bring the concepts we've been discussing in the last few chapters on the Tanakh into the New Testament—with all the implications that might provide us for interpretation. Others suggest the combination means nothing more than "*male-bedder*" or "*male-who-has-sex*" to describe a sexually-active, possibly promiscuous, man. However it's important to remember that compound words often have different meaning from their root components (e.g. "under-stand" or "chair-man"), and the meaning of a word is often unrelated to its etymology (history).

Another suggestion is that the root word choices come from this verse, but are used to directly translate the 1st century rabbinic term "*mishkav zakur*", meaning "lying with a male", into Greek. The general connotation is the same as with the first suggestion, except that it may be a broader concept than a specific reference to the one command in the Law.

There is general, though not universal, agreement that some form of male-with-male sex is being condemned by Paul in the context of his letter. The first big question for scholars and ourselves today is why did Paul choose to make up a word when he had plenty of same-sex referencing terms to select from in existing Greek and Roman vocabulary?

What would the Greeks and Romans have written?

While it is remotely possible that *arsenokoites* was a commonly-used word in conversations of the time, it's much more likely that this word is unique to Paul or the small Christian communities at the time given its complete absence in contemporary secular writings.

There were no exactly equivalent words for "homosexual" in Greek, nor in any ancient language. The English word and the entire concept behind it is very modern, having been first used in German in 1869 in a pamphlet advocating for the repeal of sodomy laws in Prussia. It was translated into English scientific literature in 1892. Before this time, there was little concept of innate binary orientation. It was generally assumed that most people could desire sex with either gender, and the terms were mostly used to describe very specific *sexual behaviors and forms of relationships*. Some terms and commentary seemed to acknowledge that certain people were more inclined to same-sex relationships than others, but that wasn't considered a requirement for the sexual activity. We also see a focus on male-with-male sex, with only one mention of female-with-female sex in the entire Bible, so broadening out to the general term "homosexuality" is not directly supported by the original languages.

There were many terms used for different aspects of either same-sex relationships or sexual acts during the time of Paul which he chose not to use in this passage. We have extensive examples from earlier Greek writers such as Herodotus, Plato, Aristotle and Plutarch. The first-century Jewish writers Josephus and Philo wrote about homosexuality, including commentary on Sodom and Gomorrah, but did not use *arsenokoites* in their work. Early Greek-speaking Christian writers like Tatian, Justin Martyr, Gregory of Nyssa and Saint John Chrysostom all wrote negatively of homosexuality, but they used different words and phrases.

Some of the available Greek words included:[28]

- *kinaidos:* an effeminate man "whose most salient feature was a supposedly feminine love of being sexually penetrated by other men."[29]
- *arrenomanes, paidomanes:* mad after men or boy crazy
- *dihetaristriai, hetairistriai, tribad, tribades, frictrix, lesbai*: synonyms referencing lesbian sexuality[30]
- *erastes* and *eromenos*: referring to partners in pederasty
- *paiderasste*: sexual behavior between males
- *paiderastes:* from *pais*, a boy, meaning lover of boys
- *paidophthoros*: corrupter of boys
- *euryproktoi*: men who dress as women, also a vulgar reference to anal penetration
- *pathikos*: the passive penetrated partner in a male couple
- *lakkoproktoi*: vulgar reference to anal penetration

Once again, we must ask why Paul felt compelled to coin a new word when he could have used any of the ones above if he meant only to condemn same-sex relationships in general.

Other uses of *arsenokoites* in Greek literature

Out of the roughly 77 times that this word is found in Koine

---

28 Indebted to Rick Brentlinger from http://bit.ly/HS-gayterms

29 "The Constraints of Desire", John J. Winkler

30 "Love Between Women", Bernadette Brooton, p. 23

Greek literature, almost all are exact copies of the vice lists in the New Testament without any additional context that would help us understand the original meaning. The few that use it independently include:

- Accusation against pagan gods as violating Roman law, at a time when same-gender relationships and sexual activity were not illegal but prostitution among the upper classes was. — Aristides (2nd century)
- Accusation included in lists of economic sins and injustice, including robbery, swindling and unjust exploitation of others. — Found in the *Sibylline Oracles*, *Acts of John* and Theophilus' *To Autolychus* (2nd to 6th century)
- Male rape/enslavement — Hippolytus (3rd century)
- A 3rd century reference by Bardesanes to behavior that was very shameful for a man, cited by Eusebius in the 4th century with added commentary that may or may not tie the behavior to having a male lover in some form.
- A despised sexual act regardless of gender: *"And many even practice the vice of arsenokoites with their wives"*. — Jonannes Jejunator (6th century)
- Accusation of pederasty between bishops and young boys. — Malalas (6th century)

Careful scholars on both sides of this debate agree that there is currently no way to conclusively define this word by referencing usage in other literature, beyond a general negative connotation largely associated with sexuality. From these sources we cannot either affirm or refute a direct connection with same-gender sexuality with full confidence.

It wasn't until the 13th century that commentators like Saint

Thomas Aquinas began to directly associate *arsenokoites* with some forms of same-sex practices (remember, not orientation), many centuries after the period when the word or the language itself was commonly used or understood.

At this stage in our study, I'm left with two questions:

1. If Paul, inspired by God, wanted to make a prohibition against all same-sex relationships and practice very clear for all time, he had other clear terms to use. Many Greek writers wrote against various forms of same-sex relationships in their culture, using a variety of explicit words and descriptive phrases. Why is something which seems so important left so ambiguous?
2. If we accept the theory that Paul derived the word *arsenokoites* from the Greek translation of Leviticus in the Septuagint, how would our prior exploration of that text as possibly referring to temple prostitution practices affect our reading of 1 Timothy 1:9-10?

Arsenokoites translations over time

As we looked at in the early chapters, every translator has to make interpretation decisions based on their expertise and research, and are always influenced (consciously or not) by their surrounding culture and colleagues. The following list shows the variety of Greek to English translation choices for *arsenokoites* throughout the years. Take particular note of the three listed revisions of the popular New International Version (NIV) to see how the same word is translated in different ways by the same group of translators over a period of just a few decades:

Bible Version	Year	Arsenokoites
Wycliffe	1382	to them that do lechery with men
Geneva Bible	1599	buggerers
King James Version	1611	them that defile themselve with mankind
Darby	1890	sodomites
Young's Literal	1898	sodomites
American Standard	1909	abusers of themselves with men
Worldwide English	1969	men who have sex with other men
The Living Bible	**1971**	**homosexuals**
New International Version	1973	perverts
New Revised Standard *	1989	sodomites
Good News Translation	1992	sexual perverts
Contemporary English *	1995	who live as homosexuals
New Living Translation *	1996	who practice homosexuality
Holman Christian Standard	1999	homosexuals
English Standard Version *	2001	men who practice homosexuality
Today's NIV *	2001	for those practicing homosexuality
New English Translation *	2006	practicing homosexuals
Expanded Bible	2011	who have sexual relations with people of the same sex [are practicing homosexuals]
New American Bible RE	2011	sodomites
New International Version *	2011	those practicing homosexuality

The marked versions above use gender-inclusive language as they determine it is appropriate for the context. Note that some decide this term only refers to men, following the original Greek word forms, and some expand the application to include women.

It seems that we have a general drift in translation from the older to the newer translations. The older translations could be seen to generally imply an abusive situation, from "*abusers of themselves with mankind*" to "*sodomites*" which could imply rape. Notice that the focus is on an action which any male might perform. This changed in the 1970's as a number of translators began interpreting the word as referring to the moral makeup or identity of a person: a pervert, or homosexual. Then in the 1990's most, though not all, changed once again to emphasize a combination of identity ("homosexual") with action ("living as" or "practicing"), as the concept of innate "same-sex attraction" began to be accepted more widely in even the conservative community.

Even if we were to accept these translators' direct connection between *arsenokoites* and homosexuality, note that translations have adjusted based on the changing understanding of our world, scientific discovery, and engagement with people in our communities. While reading the Holman Christian Standard Bible from 1999 would lead a reader to understand that Paul claims all gay people are seen in the same category as murderers and idolators by God, switching to the English Standard Version published two years later leads us to think it is only a sex act or lifestyle which is condemned. These are very different interpretations and applications of the same text.

Now that we've seen how much this word has varied in translations, it's important to return to a question of intent: is this transition a legitimate change to apply the original meaning of the text more clearly to today's culture, or is it driven by a conservative Christian ideological agenda?

Arsenokoites in Scriptural Context

Returning to our text, let's expand out from this one isolated word and look at our context.

The first epistle to Timothy

We don't have time or space to dive in deep on the entire book. Let's remember that this is a short letter from one man to another (which we Christians affirm to be inspired by God), written in a specific time and place, with a particular set of goals. This one appears to consist of general advice for the leader of an early Christian church.

Paul's main point in the introduction

Paul begins with a greeting in the name of "*God our savior and Christ our hope*", and then immediately dives into his concerns about proper teaching in the church.

His primary concern for correct teaching is love—love that comes from a pure heart, clear conscience and sincere faith. He's concerned that some have missed this goal, and started teaching about laws instead, not understanding the words or matters they assert.

He affirms the goodness of the Law, but only if used carefully to convict those who are unrighteous. He recites a list of sample behaviors that exemplify those who need the Law: criminals, rebels, the godless, the profane, those who kill their fathers and mothers and anyone else, fornicators, *arsenokoites* (often translated sodomite, which could imply rapists?), slavers/kidnappers, and liars.

Does this list seem to describe a person who is a dedicated Christian, loving God and doing good, who is or seeks to be faithfully and lovingly married to someone of the same sex? Are they in need of the Law in a way that I am not simply because I'm married to someone of the opposite sex?

What else does Paul instruct in this epistle?

If we're spending so much time on wondering how to apply one word in this Epistle, it doesn't seem reasonable to ignore the remainder of the instructions Paul gives. We should consider applying the same standard to everything else in the book, or we risk allowing the assumptions we bring to the text become tools to fit our personal agenda.

What are a few other things Paul instructs Timothy about? Well, there's quite a bit you can read on your own, so let me pull out a few topics that might help us in our discussion.

1. **Instructions for women:**
    - Dress modestly with no jewelry. (2:9)
    - Must be silent and submit in learning. (2:11)
    - Not allowed to teach or have any authority over a man... (2:11)
    - ...because man was created first and women fall to temptation... (2:13-14)
    - ...but they can be saved through childbearing if leading modest/sensible lives. (2:15)
    - Oddly, after being told not to have leadership positions, women are instructed to dignity and faithfulness in the middle of instructions about Deacons. (3:11)

- While celibacy is man's highest calling in service to God elsewhere, young widows can't be trusted to stay unmarried and righteous. (5:11-14)
2. **Everything God has created is good**
    - False teachers will come in Timothy's future, forbidding marriage... (4:3)
    - ...forbidding food. (4:3)
    - Nothing God created is to be rejected if received with thanksgiving. (4:4)
3. **Instructions for slaves**
    - Slaves should honor their masters...
    - ... and work harder for believing owners. (6:1-2)
    - No instructions given here f
    - or the slave-owners to care for the slaves in return.
4. **Polygamy** is a disqualification specifically for bishops (the "*overseers*" of pastors) in the church (3:2, 12)

I won't do much more than bring these things up, as we could spend a long time talking about them. We'll move on after pointing out two things from the brief survey:

1. I believe it's safe to assume that some of Paul's instructions were intended for a specific set of issues or environments experienced by the church of Ephesus. Certainly many faithful Christians do not consider the specific instructions about women to directly transfer to our churches today even if their denomination doesn't go so far as to ordain them. We say the same things today about the instructions to slaves, though not all Christians have always recognized that.
2. Paul seems to have a concern about those who teach

overly limiting some things, because all things created by God are good and should be enjoyed. *(Given the main topic we're discussing, it seems ironic that Paul warns against future teachers forbidding marriage, though I'm sure he wasn't thinking of same-sex marriage at the time!)*

List of related word groupings?

When doing research on this passage, I found a number of suggestions for how to figure out what Paul meant when he wrote against *arsenokoites*. The recommendation I've personally found the most straightforward and helpful comes from a 35 page booklet called *The Bible, Christianity and Homosexuality* by Justin R. Cannon. The basic idea and argument structure I'm discussing here is deeply indebted to his book, which is freely available online.

The list of immoral behaviors in 1 Timothy could be seen as isolated prohibitions, but there is an interesting pattern which could help work through the meaning of our crucial word. Let's look at the entire passage in 1 Timothy 1:8-11 and break it down. I'm going to use Young's Literal Translation here because it represents the original Greek structure more accurately:

"and we have known that the law [is] good,
if any one may use it lawfully;
having known this, that for a righteous man law is not set, but

1. for lawless and insubordinate persons,
2. ungodly and sinners,
3. impious and profane,
4. parricides and matricides, men-slayers,

5. **whoremongers, sodomites, men-stealers,**
   6. liars, perjured persons,

and if there be any other thing that to sound doctrine is adverse, according to the good news of the glory of the blessed God, with which I was entrusted."
   – 1 Timothy 1:8-11 (YLT)

Note that the list could be grouped into logical sets of related terms. Let's look at it line-by-line, observing that I've returned the terms in line 4 to the same one-word format as in the original Greek as the YLT does, but using more common English words:

1. lawless – disobedient
2. godless – sinful
3. unholy – profane,
4. father-killers – mother-killers – murderers
   (*patroloas kai metroloas androphonos*)
5. **fornicators – sodomites – slave traders,**
6. liars – perjurers

It seems reasonable to think that the sets of terms on each of the lines 1-4 and 6 may be intended to be read as related concepts. Is it possible there is some form of connection between the three individual terms in 5? Let's follow Justin Cannon's suggestion to run with this speculation for a bit. Now back to our list of various translations, in the same order, but adding the entire set of three prohibitions (since we are theorizing that there may be a relationship between them) to see how they are interpreted. The original Greek words are listed at the top:

WHAT ARE THE ARSENOKOITES IN 1 TIMOTHY?

Ver	Year	*Pornos*	*Arsenokoites*	*Andrapodistes*
WYC	1382	fornicators	to them that do lechery with men	sellers, or stealers, of men
GNV	1599	whoremongers	buggerers	menstealers
KJV	1611	whoremongers	them that defile themselve with mankind	menstealers
Darby	1890	fornicators	sodomites	kidnappers
YLT	1898	whoremongers	sodomites	men-stealers
ASV	1909	fornicators	abusers of themselves with men	menstealers
WE	1969	those who use sex in the wrong way	men who have sex with other men	those who steal people
TLB	1971	immoral and impure	homosexuals	kidnappers
NIV	1973	adulterers	perverts	slave traders
NRSV	1989	fornicators	sodomites	slave traders
GNT	1992	the immoral	sexual perverts	kidnappers
CEV	1995	sexual perverts	who live as homosexuals	kidnappers
NLT	1996	sexually immoral	who practice homosexuality	slave traders
HCSB	1999	sexually immoral	homosexuals	kidnappers
ESV	2001	sexually immoral	men who practice homosexuality	enslavers
TNIV	2001	sexually immoral	those practicing homosexuality	slave traders
NET	2006	sexually immoral people	practicing homosexuals	kidnappers
EXB	2011	who take part in sexual sins	who have sexual relations with people of the same sex [are practicing homosexuals]	who sell slaves [are kidnappers/ slave traders]

Ver	Year	Pornos	Arsenokoites	Andrapodistes
NABRE	2011	the unchaste	sodomites	kidnappers
NIV	2011	sexually immoral	those practicing homosexuality	slave traders

Let's take a closer look at the pair of outside terms to see if they can give us more insight for our uncommon center word.

Pornos (πόρνος 4205)
Strong's Exhaustive Concordance: "From *pernemi* ('to sell'); a **male prostitute** (venal: 'available for purchase'), i.e. (by analogy) a debauchee (libertine)—fornicator, whoremonger."
Thayer's Greek Lexicon: "a man who prostitutes his body to another's lust for hire, a **male prostitute**; universally, a man who indulges in unlawful sexual intercourse, a fornicator"

Andrapodistés (ἀνδραποδιστής 405)
Strong's Exhaustive Concordance: "Kidnapper, **slave trader**. An enslaver (as 'bringing men to his feet')—menstealer."
Thayer's Greek Lexicon: "a **slave-dealer**, kidnapper, man-stealer, i. e. as well one who unjustly reduces free men to slavery, as one who steals the slaves of others and sells them"

The word *pornos* has two potential meanings in Greek. It could be used to refer to a man who engaged in unlawful or immoral sex, such as with prostitutes, but its literal meaning is a male prostitute—those who are available for purchase. The word's female counterpart, *pornai*, is exclusively used to describe the lowest class of female prostitutes. Unlike the higher-class *hetaera* ("companion"), *pornai* were often slave girls sold for sex. Both *pornos* and *pornai* derive from the base "to sell".

As for the disdain for slave traders (*andrapodistés*), this would have been deeply ground into the Jewish consciousness. After all, Exodus 21:16 commands that anyone who kidnaps a person should be put to death, regardless of whether they keep or sell that person. There is no ambiguity seen in the translation of this word. It is clearly referencing those who enslave others.

Male prostitutes, "sodomites," and pimps

Now that we've looked at each word separately, let's join them back together and see what we can find.

Our first term is most literally understood to be describing a male prostitute, a man whose body is sold for sex—something forbidden by Levitical law, but available in the Roman world. Our third term is clearly depicting someone who deals in slaves.

Is it possible that *arsenokoites* specifically describes men who purchase the services of an enslaved male prostitute (*pornos*) who is owned by the *andrapodistest*? In this case, Paul could be masterfully indicting the entire immoral chain of male prostitution, bundling the three up as equally sinful acts. This might have been shocking and convicting to some Greek believers who may have assumed the only one at fault was the prostitute according to contemporary understanding.

Extra-Biblical support for enslavement concept

This connection to enslaved prostitutes would also very clearly fit the usage of *arsenokoites* to imply some form of economic crime in a few of the extra-Biblical Greek texts we have. A financial transaction for the use of a male prostitute would certainly be a form of sex-based economic exploitation:

> Never accept in your hand a gift which derives from unjust deeds.
>
> Do not steal seeds. Whoever takes for himself is accursed—to generations of generations, to the scattering of life.
>
> Do not *arsenokoitein*, do not betray information, do not murder. Give one who has labored his wage. Do not oppress a poor man. Take heed of your speech. Keep a secret matter in your heart. Make provision for orphans and widows and those in need.
>
> Do not be willing to act unjustly, and therefore do not give leave to one who is acting unjustly.
>
> — SIBYLLINE ORACLE 2.70-7.10 (TRANS. J.J. COLLINS)

Notice how the term *arsenokoitein* is used in the middle of a series of commandments against crimes which have nothing to do with sexuality at all, but are clearly concerned with actions that hurt people through economic means. The author calls out those who oppress the poor through theft, deception, murder, withholding wages and other unjust acts. Scholar Dale B. Martin argues that even those condemnations which seem to be about general morality may in fact have to do with economic injustice, concerning the withholding of grain to manipulate the markets, murder of competitors, and use of blackmail and fraud. He notes that there is a list of sexual sins later in this text, yet *arsenokoites* is placed here in the section labeled "On Justice".

This same pattern of finding *arsenokoites* in lists of economic injustices rather than in nearby lists of sexual immorality occurs in two other 2nd century Greek texts, the "Acts of John" and "To Autolychus". As Martin emphasizes in his research, these uses cannot disprove the possiblity of the word being used specifically to condemn all homosexual acts, but they do question the confidence of modern translators in rejecting other meanings.[31]

An interpretation of *arsenokoites* as referring the unjust use of a male prostitute, especially one who is enslaved and does not benefit financially in the economic transaction, would certainly support our speculation about these three words being linked together in condemnation. Once again, something we should continue condemning today.

If this is true that *arsenokoites* is an ambigious term with a range of justifiable translations into English, then why have translators consistently chosen to confidently render it as being a condemnation of all gay couples? Is it possible that this is more about enforcing traditional norms and conservative cultural expectations than strict and unbiased accuracy in translating a 2,000-year-old text?

Remember that we Christians have been known to use Scripture to reinforce our prejudices and ignorance in the past, as demonstrated in our historic support of slavery, geocentrism, and antisemitism. At minimum, we should be cautious about using this one ambigious word to condemn fellow gay Christians.

Conclusion

We will encounter *arsenokoites* in the next section on 1 Corinthians as well. We have more to learn there in a different context, and with our word paired with a new term referencing immoral behavior. For now, here's what I think we might be able to agree on what we've learned in 1 Timothy:

---

31 *Sex and the Single Savior*, Daie B. Martin, chapter 3

1. Most Greco-Roman concepts of accepted homosexual behavior that Paul and his audience would be familiar with are inherently unequal, impermanent, hold great potential for abuse, and were almost always adulterous since at least one partner was usually already in a heterosexual marriage.
2. Our central term "*arsenokoites*" is at best a word we cannot be absolutely certain of translating correctly, and in use it has ranged from describing specific abusive behaviors to homosexual orientation and identity depending on the translator.
3. Paul seems more concerned about missing the target of Love by abusing the Law through misapplying it than he is about banning specific immoral behaviors.
4. There is a reasonable case to be made that *arsenokoites* can be understood in context to refer very specifically to men who purchase the services of male slave prostitutes.

What do you think? Does 1 Timothy 1:10 still seem as unambiguously against monogamous same-sex marriage as it may have in the past? Does it seem reasonable to use this passage authoritatively against all forms of same-sex relationships today, or is there room for debate and conversation with fellow believers?

Let's see what more we may learn by looking at a similar list of immoral behaviors in 1 Corinthians.

> *"Fornicators, idolaters, adulterers,*
> *male prostitutes, sodomites,*
> *thieves, the greedy, drunkards,*
> *revilers, robbers—*
> *none of these will inherit*
> *the kingdom of God."*
> — 1 Corinthians 6:9-10

CHAPTER 7
The Effeminate & Sodomites in 1 Corinthians 6:9-10

Now that we have extensively discussed the term *arsenokoites* from 1 Timothy, we move on to the one other passage in the entire Bible where this word is used. Paul's first letter to the church in Corinth is of course the first usage chronologically, but I switched the order because we add an additional term to our investigation in this passage. This new word is *malakos* and is translated as "male prostitutes" in the NRSV above.

I've chosen to use the more traditional translation choice of "effeminate", as used in the King James Version and Young's Literal Translation, for the title of this chapter for reasons that will become clear as we continue our research.

The questions I have for this next-to-last passage are:

1. What is this new word "*malakos*", and what can it contribute to our understanding?
2. What can we learn about the usage of these lists in Paul's writing?
3. How are these words used in context, and for instruction, in the first epistle to the Corinthians?

The *malakos*

I hope you have found our exploration of the original languages helpful in our discussion so far, because we have more to come. In 1 Corinthians we find yet another controversial word which has been translated in various ways. However, this time the word is common in Greek usage of the time, and is also used in a few other verses in the Scriptures. Our discussion here will focus less on the literal dictionary definition, and more on what it might be intended to mean in context.

Malakos means "soft"

We'll get to the context later, but it's clear that we're looking at a list of behaviors which limit the "inheritance of the Kingdom" among the Godly. Here's the part of the list in Koine Greek that contains our two focus terms—both *arsenokoites* and *malakos* —along with one of the other words we looked at in 1 Timothy, *pornos* (οὔτε means "nor"):

πόρνοι οὔτε εἰδωλολάτραι οὔτε μοιχοὶ οὔτε *μαλακοὶ* οὔτε *ἀρσενοκοῖται*

The Greek word is *malakos* (μαλακός 3120), and it is clearly defined in a number of Biblical Greek dictionaries:

Strong's Exhaustive Concordance: "Of uncertain affinity; soft, i.e. Fine (clothing); figuratively, a catamite—effeminate, soft."

Thayer's Greek Lexicon: "soft; soft to the touch, and simply a soft raiment. Like the Latin mollis (Adj. soft, pliant, flexible, easily moved, gentle), metaphorically, and in a bad sense: effeminate, of a catamite, a male who submits his body to unnatural lewdness."

Mounce's Dictionary: "soft; soft to the touch, delicate. metaphor: an instrument of unnatural lust, effeminate."

Since this word is used widely outside the Bible, we can also look at more general Koine Greek dictionaries such as the Liddell, Scott, Jones Ancient Greek Lexicon (LSJ) which have a longer and more complete list of definitions based on usage in Classical Greek literature. The entire definition with literature references is available online[32], but I'll list the main ideas here:

malakos—"soft"

1. of things subject to touch: soft
   soft grassy meadows, of skin or flesh, sleep on soft bedding
2. of things not subject to touch: gentle
   soft fair words, tender youthful looks, mild, soft, faint or delicate scent, mild climate
3. of persons or modes of life: soft, mild, gentle
   easier to handle, of a fallen hero

---

32 "Malakos", LSJ, http://bit.ly/HS-malakos

a. in bad sense: soft *("attacked him somewhat feebly")*
b. faint-hearted, cowardly
c. morally weak, lacking in self-control *(not to give in from weakness or want of spirit, indulgences)*
d. of music: soft, effeminate *("tuned to a low pitch")*
e. of style: feeble
f. of reasoning: weak, loose *(to reason loosely)*
g. weakly, sickly

Wikipedia also has an entry for the root word *malakia*:

Malakia (μαλακία, "softness", "weakliness") is an ancient Greek word that, in relation to men, has sometimes been translated as "effeminacy". The contrary characteristic in men was *karteria* (καρτερία, "patient endurance", "perseverance").
— HTTP://EN.WIKIPEDIA.ORG/WIKI/MALAKIA

The literal definition of this word then, as used by the Greeks, is "soft", which is used in many different metaphorical ways just as our equivalent English word is. Our next question is, how do the writers in the New Testament use the word?

Herod Antipas, "Reed" Tiberias mint, 20 C.E.

The *non*-Malakos of John the Baptist

There are three uses of this word outside 1 Corinthians; two in Matthew 11:8 and one in Luke 7:25. Each of these uses is similar, so we'll demonstrate with the verse in Matthew:

"What then did you go out to see?
Someone dressed in *soft* robes?

> Look, those who wear *soft* robes are in royal palaces."
> — Quotation from Jesus in Matthew 11:8

In context, Jesus is speaking about John the Baptist, who is in prison at this time, to the crowds immediately after talking with some of John's followers. Apparently John had begun to doubt Jesus was the true Anointed One, and had sent representatives to ask in person. Jesus responds with an invitation to observe that *"the blind receive their sight, the lame walk, the lepers are cleansed, the deaf hear, the dead are raised, and the poor have good news brought to them"* (Matthew 11:5). Jesus claims that these are the signs that the kingdom of Heaven is being revealed on Earth, as his central prayer proclaims: *"...on earth as it is in heaven."*

Jesus turns back to the crowd from talking with John's disciples, and begins discussing John the Baptist. He asks the people what had attracted them to listen to John in the first place. Was he *"a reed shaken by the wind"*? Or *"someone dressed in soft robes"*? Both could be similar terms directly referring to King Herod[33], the one who claimed to be the legitimate leader of Israel. Herod had printed coins with the image of a reed, and he *"bent back and forth"* constantly trying to be accepted by both the religious leaders in Judaism as well as the Romans. He lived in luxury in the royal palace, wearing soft (*malakos*) robes, as one who had achieved what men would say is the goal of life.

Yet Jesus held up John in contrast, as one who is a prophet—and more than a prophet (11:9-15). Not a soft, pliable sycophant seeking affirmation from the rulers of the world, but a man of

---

33 It's possible Jesus also had in mind the description of God's judgement on Ptolemy from the Jewish historical book of 3 Maccabees, verse 2:22: *"He shook him on this side and that as a reed is shaken by the wind."*

God who confronts those rulers. John's prophetic message, wherein he "speaks truth to power", included the condemnation of Herod's divorce and subsequent remarriage to his brother's wife. This marriage was calculated to gain support of certain key Jewish leaders to solidify his Roman-derived kingship and authority to continue oppressing his own people. John stood up to Herod's immoral and power-grasping behavior, and was imprisoned and later executed for it. No bending here!

Jesus continues to express frustration with *"this generation"* (11:16-19), who insist on putting both John and Jesus into their framework of expectations for what Messiah will be instead of listening (11:15). He concludes: *"yet wisdom is vindicated by her deeds"*, which reminds me of how Matthew 7:15-20 describes identifying false prophets (by the fruits, the resulting actions or character attributes, of their teachings). This leads directly into one of Jesus's negative comparisons of the crowds to the town of Sodom in the judgement (11:23) which we looked at earlier.

Sorry to get carried away—I love studying the Gospels! In summary, the only other uses of *malakos* in the New Testament are to describe clothing that is explicitly a sign of luxury and likely also implying a certain moral weakness. The verse in Luke is in the parallel passage about John: *"What then did you go out to see? Someone dressed in **soft** robes? Look, those who put on fine clothing and live in luxury are in royal palaces."* (LUKE 7:25).

What about the Greeks?

So, the usages of *malakos* in the Gospels doesn't seem to have a direct connection to homosexuality. Maybe we can learn something from how this word was used outside of Scripture? Fortunately for our research, *malakos* was used widely in Koine Greek writing outside of Christian circles.

In "Nicomachean Ethics", published in 350 BCE, Aristotle uses the word in several ways:

> "of the dispositions described above, the deliberate avoidance of pain is rather a kind of softness [*malakia*]; the deliberate pursuit of pleasure is profligacy in the strict sense.";

> "One who is deficient in resistance to pains that most men withstand with success, is soft [*malakos*] or luxurious, for luxury is a kind of softness [*malakia*]; such a man lets his cloak trail on the ground to escape the fatigue and trouble of lifting it, or feigns sickness, not seeing that to counterfeit misery is to be miserable."

> "People too fond of amusement are thought to be profligate, but really they are soft [*malakos*]; for amusement is rest, and therefore a slackening of effort, and addiction to amusement is a form of excessive slackness."
> — Nicomachean Ethics, Loeb vol 73, VII vii 7; pg 417

Here we see *malakos* as "soft" used in a negative metaphorical way, but not having anything to do with sexuality. This fits well with the suggested usage in the Gospel of Matthew, but it's not the only way the word is used. Since the word in context in 1 Timothy is sandwiched between "male prostitutes" and "thieves" according to the NRSV, one sex-related and one not, we should also look for uses that might have more to do with sexuality.

Once again, there are many uses of *malakos* having to do with sexuality. It is certainly not restricted to general moral laxness, and was a popular term in debates and acusations about sexuality amongst Greek writers. I'll attempt a simple list of some of the ways it's used:

1. Boy Prostitutes

You'll be familiar with the basic idea from our discussion of 1 Timothy. A translation note from the New American Bible (Revised Edition) version of the Bible may be helpful here:

> "The Greek word translated as ***boy prostitutes*** [malakos] may refer to catamites, i.e., boys or young men who were kept for purposes of prostitution, a practice not uncommon in the Greco-Roman world. In Greek mythology this was the function of Ganymede, the "cupbearer of the gods," whose Latin name was Catamitus. The term translated sodomites refers to adult males who indulged in homosexual practices with such boys."
>
> – NABRE TRANSLATION NOTE ON 1 CORINTHIANS 6:19

Some young boys were castrated to keep their more feminine appearance longer. The emperor Nero (the "beast of Rome") dressed up one of his favorites in woman's clothing and married him, treating him as a wife, after castrating him. Not a very loving or consensual relationship!

2. The "Effeminate"

Any outward characteristics that seemed "feminine" in the culture were labeled as malakos. This could be anything from physical characteristics, to preferring luxury to hard work, or to be a scholar. For a male to take on any characteristics of the feminine, or even to value womanly qualities, was to reduce the assumed natural superiority of the male in the culture.

3. Womanizers

This may come as a surprise to you, because it certainly did for me. Greco-Roman culture in the first century generally looked down on men who displayed too great a love of women! Descriptions of men curling their hair, wearing perfume, and dressing up to court or seduce women are not used in a positive way. Those who sought the love of women too openly were seen as men who could not control their sexual lusts ("morally weak"), or who valued women so highly as to lose some status in the culture that held up men as uniformly superior to women.

In some Greek writings, men who sought out men (usually younger boys) for relationships were regarded as more manly and masculine, since they valued men over women. *Malakos* was an insult traded back and forth in the numerous debates about the superiority of a man loving either a woman or another man. Those who argued that male homosexual love was best made their case that to pursue a woman beyond the simple need to procreate was to taint a man with the "softness" or "effeminacy" of a woman. Men who fall in love with women demonstrate their effeminacy (*malakos*) by being controlled by women.

4. Male Prostitutes

I mentioned the three general concepts of homosexual behavior in our last section 1 Timothy, but left the last one to be explained here.

Much, thought not all, of the homosexual activity in ancient Greco-Roman culture appears to have been in pederastic and slave-prostitute environments. There are some writings that refer to adult free men who have chosen to continue relationships, either for profit/patronage or by choice. They were generally looked down on by all of society, and the word *malakos* was sometimes used as an insult for them. Some of these did choose to take on feminine clothing, hair and make-up styles.

Summary of usage in literature

There is a good case to be made that Paul was using the word *malakos* specifically for the negative sexual meaning in the Greco-Roman world. However, it was certainly not restricted to homosexuality. Men in the first century were accused of *malakos* for any of the following:

- Eating or drinking too much—enjoying luxury.
- Having long hair, shaving, wearing nice clothes (basically being a modern "metrosexual").
- Keeping knees together, or swaying when walking.
- Dancing, laughing or gesturing too much.
- Being penetrated sexually by man or woman.
- Enjoying sex with women too much—a "wanton" person.
- Masturbating.

How is *malakos* translated in various Bible versions?

While *malakos* was often seen as a euphemism for the despised ("wasteful of seed") practice of *masturbation* during the first few centuries of Christianity, it gradually shifted away from that view through the Middle Ages. Today this is not something we will see reflected in our Bible translations, even though the equivalent word in modern Greek is a common ephiphet describing masturbation today.

Let's look at a translation comparison table for both *malakos* and *arsenokoites* as used in this verse. The first three terms in the list are consistently translated "fornication/sexual immorality" (rather than the more literal "male prostitute" as just studied), "idolatry/worshipping idols" (*eidololatres*) and "adulterers" (*moichos*), so a translation comparison isn't useful on those.

Ver	Year	*Malakos*	*Arsenokoites*
WYC	1382	lechers against kind	they that do lechery with men
GNV	1599	wantons	buggerers
KJV	1611	effeminate	abusers of themselves with mankind
Darby	1890	those who make women of themselves	who abuse themselves with men
YLT	1898	effeminate	sodomites
ASV	1909	effeminate	abusers of themselves with men
WE	1969	those who commit **adultery of any kind**, who have idols	
TLB	1971	homosexuals	
NIV	1973	male prostitutes	homosexual offenders
NRSV	1989	male prostitutes	sodomites
GNT	1992	homosexual perverts	
CEV	1995	pervert	behaves like a homosexual
NLT	1996	male prostitutes	practice homosexuality
HCSB	1999	**anyone practicing homosexuality**	
ESV	2001	**men who practice homosexuality**	
TNIV	2001	male prostitutes	practicing homosexuals
EXB	2011	male prostitutes [or passive homosexual partners]	men who have sexual relations with other men [or active homosexual partners]
NET	2006	passive homosexual partners	practicing homosexuals
NABRE	2011	boy prostitutes	sodomites
NIV	2011	**men who have sex with men**	

If we consider the Greek usage of *malakos*, you might notice how the older translations seemed to do a better job bringing those literal 1st century meanings forward directly. Until the 1970s, when homosexuality became a controversy in the conservative Christian world, it was consistently translated with the connotation of "effeminancy" or "wantonness".

Just as we saw in the previous chapter, the interpretation and application of this word has changed dramatically over time.

Two becoming one

Noticd that there is considerable variation in translating *malakos* and *arsenokoites* in 1 Corinthians. The largest difference is how some choose to combine the two into a single concept, even though the Greek clearly has them as separate terms.

This is an example of the dynamic style of translation, which goes beyond a literal transfer of words in an attempt to convey the underlying ideas which the original readers might have understood. In general this is a good and necessary thing, since a 2,000 year difference goes beyond common languages. However, it also requires the translator to interpret and make theological decisions which are always influenced by current context and the inherent biases every human being has. What we should do now is ask *why* the translators have made these decisions.

Amongst the single-concept translations, we see the translators choosing meanings as varied as "those who lust for their own kind", an effeminate/womanly man (four times), male/boy prostitutes (four times) and perverts. Only one, the conservative NET Bible we discussed briefly back in chapter 1, chooses to unambiguously declare that *malakos* means "passive homosexual partners".

Since the sexual revolution in America, seven translations in our list explicitly associate this term with homosexuality (if we generously assume that's what's implied by "perverts"), and four others emphasize male prostitution. Keeping in mind that these translations are all generally conservative translations that are not going to take risks on new translation theories, note that one third choose a term that focuses on prostitution instead of broad prohibitions against gay sex.

Six translations combine both *malakos* and *arsenokoites* into a single list item, somehow deciding that they describe a single concept instead of two. That seems strange on first read since no translation I've seen has done this with *arsenokoites* in 1 Timothy. Here's how the combinations read:

- "adultery of any kind"
- "homosexuals"
- "men who have sex with men" (2011 NIV)
- "homosexual perverts"
- "anyone practicing homosexuality"
- "men who practice homosexuality" (2001 ESV)

Two have decided that this refers directly to male-with-male sex, while three broaden this to include acts between lesbians even though the words themselves are male gender. The outlier groups it all into "adultery of any kind" even though there is a Greek word for adulterers (*moichos*) appearing later in this list!

Active and passive partners

There is a specific concept underlying the decision for some translators (demonstrated by the 2011 NIV and 2001 ESV, above) to combine the two words *malakos* and *arsenokoites* into one blanket condemnation of homosexuality. That is, the first century concept of "passive and active partners".

In much of ancient Greco-Roman culture the ideas of passive and active sexual partners were more important than the physical genders of men and women. Women were "by nature" understood to be the passive partner (explicitly "the one who is penetrated"), except for some idolatrous situations that we'll look in the next section on Romans. In the common pederasty relationship we looked at in the last section on 1 Timothy, it was important in the culture to consider the young partner the passive one, and the older male would be the active partner. As the young man grew up, he would be expected to leave this passive role behind and become the active partner with a youth. Any hint of either reversing these two roles or implying equality between the two was condemned by many in the Greek culture, though not all.

We've already seen this idea in Leviticus, where men were forbidden to lie with another man (quite possibly a cult temple prostitute as we discussed) in a way that "treated him like a woman." Given the often heavily misogynistic culture, treating a man like a woman reduced his status in the society because of the believed inferiority of the gender.

Malakos was sometimes used in Greek literature to imply the passive partner, and, as we've seen, many of our current mainstream translators translate *arsenokoites* as a more active male partner. So there is some logic behind this translation. Yet, if Paul really had the two unequal partners from pederasty in mind, we would expect him to use the standard Greek word pairs of *erastes* + *eromenos* or *paiderastes* + *kinaides*. Not only does he never use these terms, but the ones used instead are separated in the list of vices exactly the same as the terms for idolatry or theft.

It seems to me that the translators of the NIV (dynamic-style translation) and ESV (literal-style translation) in particular have assumed two things in their interpretation:

1. That *arsenokoites* and *malakos* describe exclusively "active" and "passive" partners in a same-sex act.
2. And that this applies to modern same-sex relationships.

This does not seem to match our current understanding of homosexuality being an orientation toward attraction and sex that can be fulfilled in either abusive or promiscuous ways, or in a committed monogamous relationship between two equals.

Those who lack self-control

Referring back to our list of definitions of *malakos*, one other way the word was used was to indicate those who were morally weak and lacked self-control. It could refer to people who become controlled by their lusts.

We'll return to this concept in the next chapter on the passage in Romans 1 when we look at those who are described as being carried away by lusts and passions.

So, what does *malakos* mean?

The definition of *malakos* is clear but broad enough that we must consider context. It's definitely used negatively, and likely metaphorically. Any of the following are reasonable translations:

- Those who are controlled by their lust, for men or women.
- Those who are morally weak in general.

- Young male prostitutes ("*catamites*").
- Older male prostitutes who dress effeminately to continue as the "passive" partner for wealthy patrons.

It seems clear to me that the well-regarded conservative translators of the NIV (thought-for-thought style translation) and the ESV (more literal word-for-word translation) are convinced that the combination of *malakos* and *arsenokoites* refer specifically to a pederastic relationship. Accepting either the catamite or effeminate prostitute definition of *malakos* does not accurately reflect the monogamous, committed, egalitarian gay marriage ideal being proposed by some Christians today. Can we join together in agreeing with Paul and these translators that we do not want to encourage these abusive relationships between inequals, yet also understand that they have nothing to do with the question in today's world?

Paul's lists

Now that we've looked at the word *malakos* in detail, and added the various interpretation ideas in with our definition(s) of *arsenokoites*, let's look at the context of the words. The first observation is that they occur in a list of vices, similar to 1 Timothy. But these are not the only occurrences of lists in Paul's writing.

It's a list

A suggestion by Robin Scroggs in his book "*The New Testament and Homosexuality*" is that the contents of this list of immoral behaviors could have been sourced from standard lists of immorality that were circulating at the time. We even see lists like this used outside of Scripture. In other words, we could consider the possibility that the specifics on this list weren't necessarily germane to Paul's topic. He may have merely grabbed a few samples to illustrate his main point.

I've seen this concept cited in other sources as well. The Greeks had their own similar lists of morality. *The Wisdom of Solomon* in the Apocrypha of the Bible has one in chapter 14 (we'll take a quick look at this in our discussion on Romans). The first century Jewish philosopher Philo of Alexandria claimed king-of-the-hill in list-making with 147 entries in one copy!

Other lists from Paul?

We have already seen one other list in 1 Timothy, which shares the term *arsenokoites*, but not *malakos*. Obviously Paul doesn't feel that he needs to use these two words together in every list to get his meaning across, which further weakens the recent translation practice of pairing the words as one concept.

Where can we find all these lists in the New Testament? Let's pull them into our study here:

GALATIANS 5:19-21 — "Now the works of the flesh are obvious: fornication, impurity, licentiousness, idolatry, sorcery, enmities, strife, jealousy, anger, quarrels, dissensions, factions, envy, drunkenness, carousing, and things like these. I am warning you, as I warned you before: those who do such things will not inherit the kingdom of God." *(15 items)*

1 CORINTHIANS 5:10 — "I wrote to you in my letter not to associate with sexually immoral persons – not at all meaning the immoral of this world, or the greedy and robbers, or idolaters, since you would then need to go out of the world." *(4 items)*

1 Corinthians 5:11 — "But now I am writing to you not to associate with anyone who bears the name of brother or sister who is sexually immoral or greedy, or is an idolater, reviler, drunkard, or robber. Do not even eat with such a one." *(6 items)*

1 Corinthians 6:9-10 — *"Do you not know that wrongdoers will not inherit the kingdom of God? Do not be deceived! Fornicators, idolaters, adulterers, **male prostitutes**, **sodomites**, thieves, the greedy, drunkards, revilers, robbers—none of these will inherit the kingdom of God." (10 items)*

2 Corinthians 12:20 — "For I fear that when I come, I may find you not as I wish, and that you may find me not as you wish; I fear that there may perhaps be quarreling, jealousy, anger, selfishness, slander, gossip, conceit, and disorder." *(8 items)*

Romans 1:29-31 — "They were filled with every kind of wickedness, evil, covetousness, malice. Full of envy, murder, strife, deceit, craftiness, they are gossips, slanderers, God-haters, insolent, haughty, boastful, inventors of evil, rebellious toward parents, foolish, faithless, heartless, ruthless." *(20 items)*

Romans 13:13 — "Let us live honorably as in the day, not in reveling and drunkenness, not in debauchery and licentiousness, not in quarreling and jealousy." *(6 items)*

1 Timothy 1:9-10 — *"This means understanding that the law is laid down not for the innocent but for the lawless and disobedient, for the godless and sinful, for the unholy and profane, for those who kill their father or mother, for murderers, fornicators, **sodomites**, slave traders, liars, perjurers, and whatever else is contrary to the sound teaching..." (14 items)*

If we compile all the terms together and sort by frequency of use, the top ten repeated terms are:

1. Fornicators, "*porneia*" (**5 times**)
2. Drunkard/Drunkenness (**4 times**)
3. Idolatry/idolator (**4 times**)
4. Greedy (**3 times**)
5. Jealousy (**3 times**)
6. Quarrels/Quarreling (**3 times**)
7. Robbers (**3 times**)
8. Anger (**2 times**)
9. Envy (**2 times**)
10. Gossip (**2 times**)

Arsenokoites and *malakos* are after position 15 when considered by number of repetitions. Neither seem to be especially worrisome to Paul. Both pederasty and male prostitution, both harmful and immoral forms of sexual relationships were widely known in the culture at the time, yet Paul didn't spend much time on prohibitions against them.

Given the focus on homosexuality as an especially immoral identity or practice in conservative Christian circles today, it's suprising that Paul and the early church did not seem to be similarly concerned about the same-sex relationships in their culture.

The evolving of the list in 1 Corinthians

Within this one letter to the church in Corinth, we can find three of the lists, and they all seem to be related. I've complied all the listed terms in the table below so that you can see how the list grows over the three back-to-back repetitions:

I Corinthians **5:10**	I Corinthians **5:11**	I Corinthians **6:9-10**
pornos	*pornos*	*pornos*
greedy	greedy	greedy
robbers [extortioners]	robbers [extortioners]	robbers [extortioners]
idolator	idolator	idolator
	reviler	*reviler*
	drunkard	*drunkard*
		adulterers
		malakos
		arsenokoites
		thieves

Paul is using the list motif in building his argument, adding items to his list every time he repeats it. Is it possible that the list itself is not meant to be the focal point, but that it is placed here to support his main argument? What would that argument be? We'll look at that in the final part of this section.

So what can we learn from the lists?

Some Christians claim that homosexual orientation and/or practice is an especially important sin to God, either because of something inherently perverted or idolatrous, or because it tends to be something repeated without repentance, unlike something like stealing. However, even if our two somewhat ambiguous terms are condemning homosexuality as a whole, Paul certainly doesn't seem to emphasize it in his lists. Only 2 of the 6 lists include words that could possibly imply homosexuality, even though quite abusive same-gender practices were prominent in Greco-Roman culture of the time, and none of the clearest terms are ever used.

The lists seem to be used to stand in for something in an argument, not to be a focus on their own. We have to look more broadly at the text to see what is being taught.

What is Paul teaching the Corinthian church?

Paul had originally founded the church in Corinth, and apparently continued to act as an advisor at a distance through letters (this one likely written from Ephesus). This letter, like many others, was written to address specific issues of the time which we find to also be helpful in our walk today.

Outline of the letter

This sample outline comes from a conservative Christian group associated with the Dallas Theological Seminary, condensed slightly for brevity:

1. Greetings and thanksgiving (1:1-9)
2. Divisions in the Church
   a. The Fact of Divisions (1:10-17)
   b. The Causes of Division (1:18–4:13)
   c. The Cure for Divisions (4:14-21)
3. **Disorders in the Church**
   a. Failure to Discipline an Immoral Brother (5:1-13)
   b. Failure to Resolve Personal Disputes (6:1-11)
   c. Failure to Exercise Sexual Purity (6:12-21)
4. Difficulties in the Church (7:1–14:40)
   a. Concerning Marriage (7:1-40)

    b. Concerning Christian Liberty (8:1–11:1)
    c. Concerning Worship (11:2–14:40)
 5. Doctrinal Correction of the Church Regarding the Resurrection (15:1-58)
 6. Closing (16:1–24)

Section 2: Divisions in the church

It seems obvious at the beginning that Paul is writing in reaction to major divisions in the church. Members are claiming allegiance to certain teachers, and breaking the unity of the body (this sounds familiar). Paul is firm: *"Now I appeal to you, brothers and sisters, by the name of our Lord Jesus Christ, that all of you be in agreement and that there be no divisions among you, but that you be united in the same mind and the same purpose."* (1:10)

He emphasizes our equality in humbleness—not to rely on human wisdom but on the power of God. There are some, he says, who are spiritually mature, but their level of insight cannot be understood by the immature like those in this church. *"For as long as there is jealousy and quarreling among you, are you not of the flesh, and behaving according to human inclinations?"* (3:3)

> Now if anyone builds on the foundation with gold, silver, precious stones, wood, hay, straw—the work of each builder will become visible, for the Day will disclose it, because it will be revealed with fire, and the fire will test what sort of work each has done.
>
> If what has been built on the foundation survives, the builder will receive a reward. If the work is burned up, the builder will suffer loss; the builder will be saved, but only as through fire.
> — 1 CORINTHIANS 3:12-15

Our work will be judged by God, not man. Paul makes it very clear that when we think we are wise (insisting we know what the one true path is—*"following Apollos"* or *"following Paul"*), we should learn to be a fool again to attain true wisdom! (3:18)

He ends this section with a plea to stop judging: *"Therefore do not pronounce judgment before the time, before the Lord comes, who will bring to light the things now hidden in darkness and will disclose the purposes of the heart. Then each one will receive commendation from God."* (4:5) Instead he asks them to follow the examples he and Apollos are setting as humble servants. *"For the kingdom of God depends not on talk but on power [ability to perform]."* (4:20)

Section 3: Disorders in the church

Paul next addresses three specific sinful situations he's heard about in the church:

1. **A man living with his father's wife**—*"you are to hand this man over to Satan for the destruction of the flesh, so that his spirit may be saved"*. (5:5)
2. **Bringing lawsuits** against brothers in the courts instead of settling matters in the church or allowing yourself to be defrauded for the sake of unity—*"In fact, to have lawsuits at all with one another is already a defeat for you. Why not rather be wronged? Why not rather be defrauded?"* (6:7)
3. Abusing freedom in Christ by **going to prostitutes** (6:15-16)—*"'All things are lawful for me,' but not all things are beneficial. 'All things are lawful for me,' but I will not be dominated by anything."* (6:12)

It is in between the last two points that our specific verses are found. Paul makes it very clear that he is affirming our freedom from the law in Christ. There is nothing we are *forbidden* to do as part of the body of Christ, yet there are two criteria which we should apply to determine if we *should* do certain things.

We should examine if we will:

1. be **harmed** by, or harm others by, a given practice, or
2. be **controlled** by this practice.

Most Christians, liberal and conservative, would agre that participating in prostitution or sexual promiscuity is harmful or controlling (leading us away from Christ). The question is, are same-sex marriages between Christians different from heterosexual marriages in this regard? It seems we can look for signs of harm and control in the same way we would analyze traditional marriages—and we can certainly find examples of both healthy and unhealthy marriages in that environment.

Section 4: Difficulties in the church

Now let's complete our summary of 1 Corinthians, continuing on into chapter 7:

On marriage and celibacy

- Paul makes it clear that his *personal preference* (7:25) is for everyone to stay celibate like himself. He doesn't seem to be a big fan of marriage for anyone who can avoid it, at least for the specific time he was writing (*"the world as they knew it was passing away"*). (7:31)
- For those married, it must be an egalitarian relationship of mutual rights—no allowance for domination. (7:3)

- For those who cannot be at peace and live righteously in celibacy, they should marry. (7:36)

This last statement seems like it could be a good argument for the affirmation of same-sex marriage rather than a enforcement of celibacy against the wishes or abilities of individuals. Paul himself prefers celibacy for all, gay or straight, but encourages marriage as the best option for those who do not feel called to or equipped for this life-long commitment.

Food offered to idols, cultural adaptation, and freedom

- Even eating food sacrificed to idols (one of the two prohibitions requested by the Jerusalem Counsel in Acts 15) is not a sin—we should only be aware of our testimony when we partake with those who don't understand. (8:4)
- Paul has made himself conform to all cultures, and be "*all things to all people*" to bring Christ to everyone. (9:22)
- Everything is permissible, but not everything is beneficial— what will help those around us and build them up? (10:23)

Worship practices in the Corinthian church

- Women must have heads covered in prayer and prophecy, and men must not (11:4-13).
- "Does not *nature* itself teach you that if a man wears long hair, it is degrading to him, but if a woman has long hair, it is her glory?" (11:14-15)
- Do not eat the Lord's Supper unworthily, letting some go hungry while others feast—weakening the collective body as some starve. (11:21)
- Gifts are given for the diversity of the body to contribute

to the whole. We should celebrate the differences.
- Love is the greatest and most lasting gift. In the end all fades but love remains, and we will see clearly. Faith, hope and love, and the greatest is love. (13:13)
- Make sure that all spiritual practices benefit each other and those who visit. (14:26)
- No permission given for women to speak in assemblies at this time. (14:35)

Paul wraps up with a defense of the resurrection and a request for help for the churches in Galatia.

What assistance can we gain from the context?

Let's finish by looking at two concepts coming out of the full context of this letter.

First, there are a number of very clear commands in the passage which most Christians I know, including very conservative groups, have decided were limited to the context of the first-century church in Corinth. Very few theologians today require head coverings for women during prayer, different hair lengths for men and women, or silence from women in church. We are comfortable not applying them to our life today, but there is no guidance in the text itself to help us determine which are lasting.

Second, Paul seems to be quite focused on how to navigate the balance between the freedom we have from the Law (our life is no longer lived by rules and regulations) in Christ, and yet our continued need to care for others and avoid practices that would harm them. I like to think his sermon on love in chapter 13 is a guide for us here—embracing faith, hope and greatest of all love as our "rule of life":

If I speak in the tongues of mortals and of angels,
> *but do not have love,*
>> I am a noisy gong or a clanging cymbal.

And if I have prophetic powers,
> and understand all mysteries and all knowledge,
>> and if I have all faith, so as to remove mountains,
> *but do not have love,*
>> I am nothing.

If I give away all my possessions,
> and if I hand over my body so that I may boast,
> *but do not have love,*
>> I gain nothing.

Love is patient;
> love is kind;
>> love is not envious or boastful or arrogant or rude.

It does not insist on its own way;
> it is not irritable or resentful;
>> it does not rejoice in wrongdoing,
> *but rejoices in the truth.*

It bears all things,
> believes all things,
>> hopes all things,
>>> endures all things.

Love never ends.
But as for prophecies, they will come to an end;
>   as for tongues, they will cease;
>   >   as for knowledge, it will come to an end.

For we know only in part,
>   and we prophesy only in part;
but when the complete comes,
>   the partial will come to an end.

When I was a child,
>   I spoke like a child,
>   >   I thought like a child,
>   >   >   I reasoned like a child;
>   when I became an adult, I put an end to childish ways.

For now we see in a mirror, dimly,
>   but then we will see face to face.

Now I know only in part;
>   then I will know fully, even as I have been fully known.

And now faith, hope, and love abide, these three;
>   *and the greatest of these is love.*

This reminds me of the conversation Jesus had with the expert on the Law who asked him his opinion on what is the greatest of the 613 commandments recorded in the Tanakh:

> 'The first is,
> "Hear, O Israel: the Lord our God, the Lord is one;
> you shall love the Lord your God with all your heart,
> and with all your soul,
> and with all your mind,
> and with all your strength."
>
> The second is this,
> "You shall love your neighbor as yourself."
> There is no other commandment greater than these.'
> — Mark 12:29-31

When the scribe heard this, he declared it to be true, that *"this is much more important than all whole burnt-offerings and sacrifices."* (Mark 12:33)

How then do we apply the Rule of Love instead of the Rule of Law today with our gay brothers and sisters? This is an important question.

- Do we count on the knowledge passed down by others, and tell them that tradition is clear—they can never have hope to enter a loving relationship the way heterosexual couples can?
- Or can we start listening, asking questions, and watching to see if there is an inherent difference in love or harm with same-sex relationships in contrast to heterosexual marriages?

It's hard to love someone as ourselves if we don't understand what they think and feel. It's impossible to know what they think and feel if we don't listen. Listening doesn't mean we have to change our minds, or ultimately change our answers in the end. But it may change our hearts in the process to know how to respond in selfless love rather than thinking of our own agendas.

Conclusion

We've now completed looking at two out of three verses in the New Testament, and five out of the total of six in the entire Bible which are commonly thought to condemn homosexuality. Let's summarize what we looked at in 1 Corinthians:

1. The Greek word *malakos* has a clear set of definitions unlike *arsenokoites*, but a wide range of application in context. Earlier translations condemn "effeminancy" or "wantonness", while more modern translators insist on applying it to homosexuality in general.
2. Paul uses lists of vices as part of his larger arguments, possibly selecting items arbitrarily while making his point. While adultery, sexual immorality and prostitution are expanded on, *malakos* and *arsenokoites* are not.
3. Paul's teaching for church in Corinth appears to be:
    a. Encouraging unity by discouraging arguments about who is right or wrong.
    b. Emphasizing freedom in Christ while watching carefully for harm and moral captivity.
    c. Giving instructions to the Corinthian church as to proper practices for their time and place, and

making sure to remember that love (carefully defined as other-focused rather than me-focused) is greater than all other spiritual gifts, knowledge, and practices that we believe we already have.

We have just one more passage to go before we wrap up our discussion, and it's broadly agreed to be the strongest one for the traditional side of the debate. Let's see what we can learn in the Epistle to the Romans.

> *"God gave them up to degrading passions.*
>
> *Their women exchanged natural intercourse for unnatural, and in the same way also the men, giving up natural intercourse with women, were consumed with passion for one another.*
>
> *Men committed shameless acts with men and received in their own persons the due penalty for their error."*
> — Romans 1:26-27

CHAPTER 8
Unnatural Acts in Romans 1:26-27

Our last text is also the one that seems to be the clearest condemnation of homosexual activity. Of all verses in the Bible, it is the only one that could possibly refer to lesbians in the original language. There are no words that are difficult to translate, even if we might need to look at interpretation and meaning in context, and the passage is clearly part of the new covenant that applies to Christians. This single verse has stopped many Christians from affirming their LGBT brothers and sisters in relationships, from conservative Christian ethicist scholar William Hays to myself for a long time.

Yet, by now you may agree with me that many texts which on the surface seen clear and unambiguous can take on new meanings and alternative valid interpretations as we study them carefully. Let's do one more word study on a peripheral term, and then spend some time trying to figure out what the apostle Paul is teaching his readers (and through that, us). Here are the questions:

1. Laying aside our prior assumptions, what could Paul be describing as natural and unnatural intercourse?
2. What is Paul teaching in Romans overall?
3. What is the intent of these verses, and of the immediate passage in the historic context?

"Natural" Intercourse

A pivotal word in the Romans text is *physikós* (φυσικός 5446) which is unambiguously translated as "natural" according to Strong's: "'physical', i.e. (by implication) instinctive:—natural." However, what does "natural" describe in Paul's context? For that we need to look at the root word *physis* (φυσικός 5449).

Understandings of *physis* in ancient Rome

Strong's defines *physis* as: "nature. growth (by germination or expansion), i.e. (by implication) natural production (lineal descent); by extension, a genus or sort; figuratively, native disposition, constitution or usage—(man-)kind, nature(-al)."

Thayer's Greek Lexicon is a little more detailed:

1. **the nature of things**, the force, laws, order, of nature; as opposed to what is monstrous, abnormal, perverse: that which is contrary to nature's laws, against nature; as opposed to what has been produced by the art of man: the natural branches, i. e. branches by the operation of nature, , contrasted with what is contrary to the plan of nature; as opposed to what is imaginary or fictitious: "who are gods not by nature, but according to the mistaken opinion of the Gentiles"; nature, i. e. natural sense, native conviction or knowledge, as opposed to what is learned by instruction and accomplished by training or prescribed by law, guided by their natural sense of what is right and proper
2. **birth, physical origin** (*"who by birth is 'uncircumcised' or a Gentile"*)
3. a mode of feeling and acting which **by long habit has become nature**
4. the sum of **innate properties and powers** by which one person differs from others, distinctive native peculiarities, natural characteristics

We can also see how it was used in the classical Greek literature context in the Liddell, Scott, Jones Ancient Greek Dictionary:

1. **Origin:** of persons, birth (e.g. not adoption); growth
2. Natural form:
    a. The natural form or constitution of a person or thing as the result of growth
    b. Nature, constitution
    c. Form or appearance, **either in mind or outward**
    d. Medical: constitution or temperament, **natural**

place or position of a bone or joint
  e. The mind: **one's nature or character**, animal instinct
  f. Natural weakness, "*i.e. wouldn't provoke a stone*"
3. Regular order of nature: growing naturally, a traitor by nature, by nature, **naturally**
4. In philosophy:
   a. **"Nature" personified as an originating power**, principle of growth in the universe, inner fire of preservation and growth in plants and animals
   b. Elementary substance: **atoms**
   c. **The creation**: heaven and earth, light and darkness
5. **Concrete identity:** Creature, mankind, womankind, of plants or material substances
6. **Species:** kind, sort, species, group or class of plants
7. **Sex:** the physical characteristics of sex, such as testes

The description of intercourse as "natural" then has a variety of possible interpretations. It could be used to designate:

- Intercourse which is consistent with the created order.
- Intercourse for procreation only (excluding anal or oral sex, masturbation, or use of any contraception methods).
- Intercourse which does not conform to cultural standards or tradition.
- Intercourse which is against the individual characteristics of a person.

Dr. James V. Brownson, Professor of New Testament at Western Theological Seminary and author of *Bible, Gender, Sexuality*, points out that the idea of "nature" as described here is a Greek concept rather than a Hebrew one. The word *physis* cannot be found in the Greek version of the Tanakh, and it only began to appear in later Jewish writings around 200 BCE as the Hebrews encountered Greek philosophy. In particular, use of this word came as Jewish philosophers began engaging with Stoicism, so to understand how Paul would have used this word we'd need to know a little about how the Stoics thought of *physis*.

The Stoic philosophy of nature

Stoicism is a Greek school of philosophy originating with Zeno of Citium around 300 BCE. By the first century it had become the most popular worldview amongst the educated elite in the Greo-Roman world and remained so for several centuries. We know that the Apostle Paul was familiar enough with Stoicism to have long debates with philosophers in Athens:

> While Paul was waiting for them in Athens, he was deeply distressed to see that the city was full of idols. So he argued in the synagogue with the Jews and the devout persons *[familiar with Scripture]*, and also in the marketplace every day with those who happened to be there *[engaging with Greeks]*. Also some Epicurean and Stoic philosophers debated with him.
> — Acts 17:16-18a

It would make sense for him to use Greek philosophical concepts for both the Gentiles and the Jews in his church audience who were living in the heart of Rome. His letter begins with an insistence that God's truth is revealed outside of Scripture as well, knowing that he can't count on the same level of familiarity with the sacred texts to make his points in this context.

For Stoics, "living in agreement with *nature*" is the means to flourishing or living well in virtue which for them is the ultimate goal of human life. They recognized the instinctual characteristics of the plant and animal world, but insisted that man's unique ability of reasoning was our true nature. They sought to overcome thoughtless passions which control us so we may gain mastery over our instincts and live with purpose and control. They believed that we could study the world and understand what it means to be in harmony with the cosmic nature.

Paul begins his letter with this very theme:

> Ever since the creation of the world his eternal power and divine nature, invisible though they are, have been understood and seen through the things he has made.
> — ROMANS 1:20

He goes on to say that the wicked have not honored God in spite of his revelation through creation, but chose instead to follow idols and thereby were given over to be controlled by their "*degrading passions*" (1:26). Stoics thought of passion very differently than we often do today. Rather than thinking of a "passionate" person as being one who is fully alive as themselves, they considered them negatively "passive"—under the control of something outside themselves. It was an excess of passion that was the problem for both Greek and Jewish philosophers like Philo. Stoics seek harmony, balance, and self-control.

In Roman society there was suspicion of anyone who indulged too much in human appetites. "Unnatural intercourse" could describe someone who was had no self-discipline or restraint but was controlled by the "lusts of their hearts" (1:24). It was a common understanding in Roman society that for many men, wives were for generating progeny and adulterous male or female love affairs were for sexual fulfillment. Rather than be content in their marriages, they would be controlled by their passions toward affairs and orgies.

Dr. Brownson suggests that by cross-referencing both the works of Paul and the larger body of Stoic literature we'll end up with three complementary uses of "nature" which combine together for a full vision of the word. These three are:

1. Individual disposition: do what comes naturally to you as a unique person.
2. Social flourishing: living for communal well-being, with agreed on values and social conventions.
3. Harmony with creation: living according to natural human patterns and needs.

Let's keep these three elements of nature in mind as we look further into how Paul uses the word in his writing.

How is *nature* used throughout the New Testament?

Unlike in the Greek translation of the Tanakh, Paul and other New Testament writers use *physis* in a number of ways (English translation indicated in bold):

> ROMANS 2:14-16 — "When Gentiles, who do not possess the law, do **instinctively** [*"by nature"*] what the law requires, these, though not having the law, are a law to themselves. *They show that what the law requires is written on their hearts*, to which their own conscience also bears witness; and their conflicting thoughts will accuse or perhaps excuse them on the day when, according to my gospel, God, through Jesus Christ, will judge the secret thoughts of all."

> ROMANS 2:27 — "Then those who are '**uncircumcised by**

nature' [*not born into the people identified by "circumcision", i.e. the Jews*] but keep the law will condemn you that have the written code and circumcision but break the law."

Romans 11:22 — "For if God did not spare the **natural** branches [*unbelieving Israelites*], perhaps he will not spare you."

Romans 11:24 — "For if you [*Gentiles*] have been cut from what is **by nature** a wild olive tree and grafted, **contrary to nature**, into a cultivated olive tree [*Jewish promise*], how much more will these natural branches be grafted back into their own olive tree."

1 Corinthians 11:13-15 — "Judge for yourselves: is it *proper* for a woman to pray to God with her head unveiled? Does not **nature itself** teach you that if a man wears long hair, it is *degrading* to him, but if a woman has long hair, it is her glory? For her hair is given to her for a covering."

Galatians 2:15 — "We ourselves are Jews **by birth** [nature] and not 'Gentile sinners'."

Galatians 4:8 — "Formerly, when you did not know God, you were enslaved to beings that **by nature** are not gods."

Ephesians 2:3 — "All of us once lived among them [the disobedient in verse 2] in the *passions of our flesh*, following the desires of flesh and senses, and we were **by nature** children of wrath ["*impulse, passions, anger*"], like everyone else."

James 3:7-8 — "For every **species** of beast and bird, of reptile and sea creature, can be tamed and has been tamed by the **human species**, but no one can tame the tongue—a restless evil, full of deadly poison."

2 Peter 1:4 — "Thus he has given us, through these things, his precious and very great promises, so that through them you may escape from the *corruption that is in the world because of lust*, and may become participants of the **divine nature**."

What can we learn from these uses of the word nature?

We can see the following meanings used in the verses above:

- An inborn conscience (*"the Law within our hearts"*).
- Birthright or genetic origin of those born as Jews.
- Cultural convention, e.g. hair lengths for men and women.
- The divine nature of God, contrasted to that of the world which is corrupted by *"lust, impulse, passions, anger"*.
- Created species, referring to both animals and man.

Other than the reference to hair length, all of these have to do with innate created characteristics that cannot be chosen. Our species, birthright, and natural inclinations are part of how God created us and desires us to participate in, contrasted to the corruption that comes from the world through lust.

Stoic *nature* principle one: Individual Disposition

Looking at the principles of nature for Stoics, let's look at how individual disposition might be considered in this context. This first concept focuses on a unique person with particular needs and interests. While there are both communal and universal components to nature, Stocism also takes into account the variations among human beings.

Let's look back at the very core verses of the passage we're currently studying with this meaning in mind:

> Their women exchanged *natural* intercourse for *unnatural*, and in the same way also the men, giving up *natural* intercourse with women, were consumed with passion for one another.
> — ROMANS 1:26B-27A

A focused reading of this sentence specifically describes women and men apparently choosing to *exchange* or *give up* intercourse that came naturally to them for something that is unnatural. Now that we know Paul is most likely referencing the common understanding of Stoic principles, his audience might well understand this word to have an individual disposition aspect to it. If at least part of his meaning is contained within this concept then it does not line up well with the modern traditional position. There seems to be a choice here, which is not the experience that our gay brothers and sisters describe. In fact, choosing against what gay individuals understand to be their unchosen nature from birth would be for them to enter into *opposite-sex* relationships.

If we accept as true that being gay is part of the diversity of God's created order, then this is a logically supportable reading even as it doesn't fully explain away the assumed condemnation satisfactorily. Let's look at the other two aspects of Stoic nature.

Stoic *nature* principle two: Social Convention

When I think of "natural" and "unnatural" acts in my language and culture, I immediately think of things that are against the created order. However, remember that in the Greek context this could have more a "custom" or "normal" connotation. We have examples of describing someone as having an "unnatural" stomach ache because it was particularly painful and outside "normal" experience, or using the word to describe social or cultural conventions.

Paul writes in the first letter to the Corinthians how "*nature [physis] itself* teaches you that if a man wears long hair, it is degrading to him, but if a woman has long hair, it is her glory" (1 CORINTHIANS 11:14-15). I've always been puzzled by this statement. It seems to me that the created "nature" of my hair is that it would be quite long if I didn't cut it. It makes more sense if Paul is talking nature in the Stoic sense of a cultural standard, as it existed in the 1st century Greco-Roman context. After all, those Hebrews who were dedicated to God's service as Nazarites several centuries before this period were specifically commanded to keep their hair long, and Paul himself took a Nazarite vow for a time. Apparently the expectation of how to honor God with your hairstyle seems to change with the culture.

In contrast to earlier Semitic cultures, 1st century Roman gender roles expected short hair for men and long hair for women. Elaborate hairstyles emphasized both the erotic nature of women's hair in their society, as well as showed off how wealthy one was (showing how many hours you could afford to spend having it groomed daily). These conventions are reflected in other epistles, requiring women to wear veils and forbidding shaved heads (1 CORINTHIANS 11:15) and cautioning against elaborate hairstyles (1 PETER 3:3).

Men who wore their hair long or styled like women could be considered either shamefully ("degrading") effeminate (possibly labeled *malikos*) or overly sensual and controlled by their passions. Either would be "unnatural" for their society.

While it's true that to be in relationship or have sex with the same gender has long been considered "unnatural" in western societies (though scholars debate how universal this really has been through the centuries), having this aspect of Stoic *physis* in mind does not support the traditional condemnation of same-sex relationships for all time. Now that we're recognizing the general principle that 5-10% of the earth's population of humans has always been drawn to the same gender from birth, we may wonder just how much of our theology around gender roles and sexual orientation has come from social convention of a given time rather than eternal principles of nature.

For Paul to condemn at least some same-sex relationships at least partially on the grounds of cultural convention at the time is something that we might today see in the same light as his writings against long hair for men. We might consider if there is an underlying principle that we can benefit from while understanding that the actual instruction came out of his human context in first century Roman culture.

Stoic *nature* principle three: Human Nature

The final aspect of Stoic *physis* to consider is the universal human order of creation. One of the most common assumptions in conservative circles is that Paul must be referring to homosexuality being uniformly "unnatural" in God's creation. And in fact this was a common and unchallenged belief until the last few decades.

Today researchers tell us that same-gender sexual attraction, sexual activity, and even life-long pairing is found consistently throughout the created world. Biologist, linguist and author Dr. Bruce Bagemihl describes studies of over 450 different species engaging in same-gender sexual activity in his book *Biological*

Exuberance: Animal Homosexuality and Natural Diversity. So far no species that reproduces sexually has been observed to be exclusively heterosexual. This publication was cited by the American Psychiatric Association and other groups in their successful efforts to strike down sodomy laws in *Lawrence v. Texas* before the Supreme Court.

Here are a few examples outside the human species:

- Approximately 10% of rams mate exclusively with other male sheep. 20% more are bisexual and 15% asexual. Studies have shown these preferences are consistent regardless of access to genders or efforts to change it.
- One-quarter of all black swan couples are between males, who will steal eggs from other nests and raise the chicks. Cygnets raised in these pairings have a better rate of survival than in heterosexual couples.
- Penguins have been observed to create permanent same-sex pairings since 1911, although that early study was so shocking to the culture at the time that the researchers translated it into Greek and passed it around in secret for the next 100 hundred years (finally published in 2012)!
- A huge variety of species have same-gender sex without exclusive pairing. For primates such as bonobos and Japanese macaques and other mammals like giraffes the majority of encounters are same-sex liaisons (lesbian and gay, respectively).

It is impossible to claim that homosexual activity is not part of natural creation from these studies. Sex is used across the created world for procreation, companionship, peace-making, domination, and social cohesion in all combinations of genders.

This includes both promiscuous and random sex, and exclusive monogamous pairings depending on species. Humans are no exception either in variety of orientation or in particular forms of sexual coupling.

I am not proposing that we should look to animals for sexual ethics. However, it is important to recognize that homosexuality is a normal innate pattern throughout creation. This would not necessarily be a concept that Paul was familiar with because it was not a common idea in the first century (though not completely unknown). If you recall our examples in the 2nd chapter of this book, remember that Scripture often reflects the scientific understanding of the age in which it was written, and it would not be out of the normal pattern for Paul to describe sexual relationships according to the norm he knew at the time.

There is one more element to the Stoic vision of *physis* in the created order aspect which might be reflected in this passage. Both the Jewish Philo and the Roman Cicero emphasized procreation as an essential part of sexuality. They considered it natural to propagate the species, and therefore might call any sexual act which would not produce progeny unnatural. This would include masturbation, anal or oral sex with any gender, or even sex with contraception in any form. This would not necessarily mean that this acts were "immoral", but they would be "unnatural" for the intent of procreation.

On this note, let's look at this line one more time: "Their women exchanged *natural* intercourse for *unnatural*..." (ROMANS 1:26B) While the initial read in connection to the rest of the sentence immediately makes most conservatives think that this is the only verse in the entire Bible which condemns lesbian relationships, note that a careful read does not say that women were having sex with other women. It simply says that they had exchanged "natural" for "unnatural" intercourse. According to Dr. Brownson, for the first few hundred years of the church this verse was understood to condemn all sex acts not considered "normal", but no one thought it had anything specific to do with lesbians. For the purposes of the culture this could have been any sex act which would not produce children.

Once again, today most of us in our society would not condemn every sex act which does not produce children as "unnatural". Contraception of various forms are considered a normal and healthy practice within a marriage. Now that we don't think male sperm contains the entirety of a human being the way people did until the 1870's, we no longer consider non-procreative ejaculation in the same vein as aborting children.

We also know much more about procreation and sexuality, and have more diverse marriages already. There are estimates that 1 child out of every 1,500 to 2,000 births qualify as "intersex" which often means sterility. We do not prevent them from marrying even though we know there is no chance they will have children. Others go through radiation for cancer treatments, or are post-menopausal at marriage, or choose not to have children with permanent contraception, or any number of different scenarios which prohibit natural childbirth as an outcome of sexual intercourse. In addition, we have more need for adoptions than we have couples willing to adopt, and we're in no danger of dying out as a species due to lack of procreation.

I do not believe we can condemn same-sex relationships on the grounds that they are inherently non-procreative when we allow so many other relationships for love and companionship.

Summarizing *nature*

While the word *physikós* is clearly translated into English as describing things which are according to *physis*, I think we've been able to see that the typical interpretation of the word in our current context may not match that of Paul's original audience. Once we look at this passage through the lens of the shared understanding of Stoicism Paul would have relied on to give him access to speak into the culture, we may see that applying those same three lens today may lead us to different conclusions.:

1. Now that we know, unlike the 1st century population, that one aspect of individual created disposition is sexual orientation, it could be seen as *natural* for some people to prefer same-sex relationships.
2. Now that social conventions are changing, it is no longer so against cultural norms to have miss-matched gender role hairstyles or to be gay.
3. Now that we understand that same-sex relations are natural for the entirety of the studied creation and we are generally comfortable having sex which will not lead directly to new progeny, sex outside of unprotected heterosexual vaginal intercourse is no longer called unnatural.

One aspect of nature from Stoicism might still apply today, however. At the beginning of this section you may recall that we briefly covered the philosophy's suspicion of and disdain for uncontrolled passions and lusts. At the root, Stoics thought that developing self-restraint, contentment with what you have, and avoiding being controlled by your desires were key to the good life.

While many Romans did not see anything inherently

harmful about same-sex relationships, they looked with disdain on those men who did not act with restraint and moderation in their sexuality. They might criticize men seeking male lovers simply because these relationships were typically adulterous, in addition to their marriage to a woman, and a sign that the man could not control his lusts. Many first century writers, both Greo-Roman and Judeo-Christian, saw the desire for same-sex relationships as an *uncontrolled excess* of the same sexual desire that a man had for his wife, rather than of a different order entirely:

> The man whose appetite is insatiate in such things, when he finds there is no scarcity, no resistance, in this field, will have contempt for the easy conquest and scorn for a woman's love, as a thing too readily given—in fact, too utterly feminine—and will turn his assault against the male quarters, eager to befoul the youth who will very soon be magistrates and judges and generals, believing that in them he will find a kind of pleasure difficult and hard to procure.
>
> — Dio Chrysostom, 1st century Greek philosopher

Note the misogyny inherent in this idea that the love of a woman is too easy to obtain, and that it is natural for a man who cannot control his "appetite" sexually to seek a challenge in obtaining a male lover. The condemnation is not of same-sex relations in general, but of a lack of self-control and restraint.

We as Christians agree that we are called to seek transformation in Christ away from the temptations of the world to indulge in harmful lusts. We may affirm this aspect of Paul's shared emphasis with the Stoics while coming to a new understanding of how not all same-sex relationships come from an excess of lust and uncontrolled passions.

We've covered this one word in detail, but there is far more in the passage than *nature*. Let's continue on to the broader context.

Putting the verses into context: the Epistle to the Romans

The Letter to the Church in Rome is the central book of the entire Bible in some schools of theology. It's certainly very important for our Christian faith, and it's been studied and written about by prominent theologians for centuries. In other words, there's no way I can do the entire book justice here, yet I think we have to know more about the intent of the epistle to understand our central verses properly.

Please bear in mind that our reading of the book may be different from your background, since there so many strong viewpoints on it. Rest assured that I did not come up with all this myself. I've studied a variety of viewpoints in addition to my own readings of the text. Regardless, maybe there's something new here that could add to your understanding in general anyway, as a side benefit to our exploration of the topic at hand?

What was going on in Rome?

Once again, we're looking at a letter, written to a specific group of people, in a specific time, at a specific place, with a specific need in mind. What can we learn about this?

Relying on some teachings from prominent New Testament scholar N.T. Wright, who holds to the traditional perspective on homosexuality by the way, the church in Rome was going through some tough times. All Jews had been kicked out of the city by the Emperor Claudius in 49 CE for being annoying proselytizers, and when they returned five years later the Christians among them found the Gentile Christians were naturally running the show. This set up a conflict between the two groups, Jews and Gentiles, over leadership capacity and examples of righteous living.

In general, the Jews felt that they were on a higher order spiritually than all other nationalities, because they had the Law and rejected the worship of idols. The Hellenistic Jewish theologians based out of Alexandria in particular seemed to have made this perceived innate difference an important distinction in their teaching.

However, the Roman Gentile Christians, who likely started as "God-fearers" in Judaism before hearing the Gospel, were also naturally adamant to maintain their new-found independence from the Law, while the returning Jewish Christians continued to keep the practices of the Law and wanted the Gentiles to join back in. The Gentiles connected the practices of the Law with the initial Roman attention and banishment, and besides didn't want to take on all these practices since things seem to have been going well without them.

Paul hears about the conflict and disagreements, and even though he's never visited the Roman church at this point, he feels that he needs clarify the gospel for a mixed audience including both Greeks familiar with Stoicism and Jews influenced by contemporary Jewish teachings and philosophy. He may also be hoping to make Rome his new missionary base, and wants a unified church to support him there.

Paul writes a letter

He begins with a fairly standard introduction, expressing his interest in coming to Rome soon. Let's run through a quick outline of the rest of the letter based on Wright's scholarship:

1. Greeting and thanksgiving (1:1-1:17)
2. The Law grants nothing special for the Jews because *the covenant is through faith and grace, not ancestry or works of the Law* (CHAPTERS 1-4)
   a. Jewish-style critique of Gentile paganism—*idols and immorality* (1:18-32)
   b. Turning this critique back on the now cheering Jewish Christians in equal blame (2:1-29)
   c. Yet God must be faithful to his covenant – but this comes through Christ, not the nation of Israel. No longer is it based on the faithfulness of men, but of Jesus. (CHAPTER 3)
   d. Therefore Abraham is our father in faith, not in flesh. Works of the law (like circumcision) have no part, only faith, hope and grace (CHAPTER 4)
3. The full restoration of all creation has been fulfilled in Christ, and the *covenant promises of the Jews are now given to all believers.* (CHAPTERS 5-8)
4. This transition from national promise to promise by faith was *always God's intent, and not a failure toward or by Israel.* Jews are welcomed equally with Gentiles, not rejected. (CHAPTERS 9-11)
5. Now the church must *live in unity*, and not risk threats *by either making moral or political errors.* Unity requires agreeing to remain in diversity. (CHAPTERS 12-16)

Thoughts on the points Paul is making

There appears to be a major conflict in the church between the Jews and the Gentiles over the Law and covenant promises. The Jews claim innate superiority based on their genetics ("*nature*") from Abraham and the giving of the Law. Paul points out that the Law has not made them morally superior, and that all are now considered equal in Christ.

He insists that they live in unity, and gives them guidance on how to live morally without needing the strictures of the Law.

In chapters 13 through 15, Paul emphasizes love and not judgement as our guiding principles.

> Owe no one anything, except to love one another;
> for the one who loves another has fulfilled the law.
>
> The commandments, "You shall not commit adultery; You shall not murder; You shall not steal; You shall not covet"; and any other commandment, are summed up in this word, "Love your neighbor as yourself."
>
> Love does no wrong to a neighbor;
> therefore, love is the fulfilling of the law.
> — Romans 13:8-10

Paul is using the words of Jesus to establish a new way of judging moral codes, laws and to determine what behaviors we should regard as sin. Instead of following a list of rules without question, we are always to ask ourselves: *"is this truly, deeply, loving my neighbor?"*

> Why do you pass judgment on your brother or sister?
> Or you, why do you despise your brother or sister?

> For we will all stand before the judgment seat of God.
> — ROMANS 14:10

This sounds similar to what we found in 1 Corinthians, and reminds me also of words Jesus spoke. Love, unity and not judging are common themes throughout the New Testament.

Back to our text: The big open

Ok, now that we've looked at one take on an overall theme for Romans, what about our core passage and the message about homosexuality? Let's take a closer look at the first two chapters.

Paul's masterful rhetoric

As we've established, Paul needs to put Jew and Gentile on the same moral plane before he can show them how they are equal in Christ. Instead of a straight-forward statement of this fact, he employs a clever rhetorical device for maximum impact (it reminds me of the prophet Amos, but that's another book!):

1. *Paul ends his greetings, stating his calling to bring the Gospel to Jews and Gentiles equally.*
2. Yet in verse 1:18 he begins to build **a case against the pagans** (identified as "*they*", the other):
    a. *They* could see God in creation, yet did not acknowledge him.
      b. "So *they* are **without excuse**"
    c. *They* exchanged the glory of God for images of men and beasts – **idols**
        d. *Because of their idolatry*, God gave them to serve the creature not the creator

e. *Because of their idolatry*, God gave them up to abandon natural sex for unnatural
   f. *Because of their idolatry*, God gave them up to all immorality and wickedness
3. Then Paul throws the trap on the Jewish believers (identified as "*you*") who were likely feeling pretty superior by now:
4. "**Therefore *you* have no excuse,** whoever *you* are, when *you* judge others; for in passing judgment on another *you* condemn *yourself*, because *you*, the judge, **are doing the very same things**." (2:1)

That is, Paul points out that the Jews also participate in the immorality and wickedness of the world, even though they have the genetics ("*nature*"), the Law, and have not been worshipping idols.

There's one more potential level to this trap though which we might immediately recognize if we lived in the 1st century too. It's a fascinating parallel, either way we interpret it, so let's do a cross-reference outside of the strict Protestant canon.

The Wisdom of Solomon

As part of the Christian tradition, inherited from our Jewish fore-fathers in faith, we have a number of extra books that are not considered by most Protestants to be at the same level of Scripture as the 66-book canon. We call these the *Apocrypha*. Martin Luther first moved them to a separate section of the Bible in 1534, but up until the early 19th century all Christians—Roman Catholic, Orthodox, and Protestant—had them all bound into the same Biblical volume. In 1826 the

National Bible Society of Scotland led the charge to remove them all from published Protestant Bibles, and until the 1960s the American and British Bible Societies follwed in banning their publication. While these prohibitions are now over, many evangelical Christians do not consider them part of the Bible, nor are they often read personally or corporately.

Although we may not hold them to the same level of inspiration and authority as the rest of the canon, we can still learn from them. We can especially gain insight into the history and mindset of the Jewish community around the time of Paul since the books were written close to this period.

While we can't know for sure if Paul read the Apocryphal book *The Wisdom of Solomon* (also know as the *Book of Wisdom* or just *Wisdom*), it's very likely that he would be familiar at least with the general arguments being made from the Hellenistic Jewish center of Alexandria. There is one section of this book, in chapters 13 through 15, that is well worth reading in the context of our exploration of Romans 1.

I've taken the text below from the well-regarded New Jerusalem Bible translation available online (it's a Roman Catholic translation, but many Protestants like it too). There are various other translations freely available online too. I'm simply going to bring out some points that help us with Romans.

In this section of Wisdom, the author builds a case against the "*they*" of the idolatrous nations. I have put key words and phrases in italics, which you may find have interesting parallels with our text in Romans:

"Yes, naturally stupid are all who are unaware of God, and who, *from good things seen, have not been able to discover*

Him—who-is, or, *by studying the works, have not recognized the Artificer...*

"And if they have been impressed by their power and energy, let them deduce from these how much mightier is he that has formed them, since through the grandeur and beauty of the creatures we may, by analogy, contemplate their Author.

"Small blame, however, attaches to them, for perhaps they go astray only in their search for God and their eagerness to find him; familiar with his works, they investigate them and fall victim to appearances, seeing so much beauty.

"But even so, *they have no excuse*: if they are capable of acquiring enough knowledge to be able to investigate the world, how have they been so slow to find its Master?

"But wretched are they, with their hopes set on dead things, who have given the title of gods to *human artifacts, gold or silver, skillfully worked, figures of animals, or useless stone*, carved by some hand long ago.

"...The idea of *making idols* was the *origin of fornication*, their discovery corrupted life...

"With their child-murdering rites, their occult mysteries, or their *frenzied orgies* with outlandish customs, they no longer retain any purity in their lives or their marriages, one treacherously murdering another or wronging him by *adultery*. Everywhere a welter of blood and murder, theft and fraud, corruption, treachery, riot, perjury, disturbance of decent people, forgetfulness of favors, pollution of souls, *sins against nature*, disorder in marriage, *adultery and debauchery*.

> *"For the worship of idols with no name is the beginning, cause, and end of every evil."*

Now the author switches to contrast the "*we*" of the Israelites:

> "But you, our God, are kind and true, slow to anger, governing the universe with mercy.
>
> *"Even if we sin, we are yours, since we acknowledge your power, but we will not sin, knowing we count as yours.*
>
> "To know you is indeed the perfect virtue, and to know your power is the root of immortality. *We have not been duped* by inventions of misapplied human skill, or by the sterile work of painters, by figures daubed with assorted colors, the sight of which sets fools yearning and hankering for the lifeless form of an unbreathing image.
>
> *"Lovers of evil and worthy of such hopes are those who make them*, those who want them and those who worship them."

How does this connect to Romans 1-2?

Notice the two-part structure and content of the argument from the author of Wisdom. Look for the similarity in the first half to Romans 1:18-32, and then note where it diverges:

1. **Indictment against *they* (all other nations).**
    a. *They* are stupid to not recognize God from creation.
    b. *They* have no excuse.
    c. *They* instead begin making idols.
    d. The author insists that *their* idols are the origin of fornication.
    e. ...leading to *their* rites of orgies, abandon-

ing marriages.
   f. ...which lead to all kinds of wickedness.
   g. To conclude, the worship of idols *they* do is the beginning and cause of all evil.
2. **In contrast, *we* the people of Israel are not like *them*.**
   a. *We* know God.
   b. Because *we* acknowledge God, *we* don't sin.
   c. Because *we* know God, *we* are not tricked by idol-makers.
   d. *They* are all lovers of evil, unlike *us*.

Have you spotted the initial striking parallel, and then the abrupt difference?

It seems to me that Paul is using Wisdom's argument, well-known to the Jews in Rome, only to destroy it in the second half (similar to how Job's friends present false concepts of God and reward for the wicked, only for him to counter them). He appears to initially accept the premise that idolatry is the root of all evil, and that the unstained (recent generations of) Jews are therefore more *naturally* righteous than idol-tainted Greeks.

Yet when Paul switches to speaking to Israel in Romans 2:1, he tips his hand. This is a ridiculous argument, he says. If worshipping physical idols, especially in sexual rituals, is the sole origin of sin, then why do the Jews also sin? No, he says, there is nothing different between the Jews and Gentiles. We are equal before God!

We could speculate and say that maybe idolatry is the root of Israel's problem as well—but instead of an idolatry of physical sculptures, they have made the Law and their 613 Commandments into the idol. The revelation of God in the Law, and practices such as circumcision that come from it, are so important that they "make Israel sinless by *nature*" (according to Jewish thought). They supposedly make those descended from Abraham morally superior, and allow them to judge others. But Paul points out their faulty foundation.

How often do we as Christians make our personal moral codes and tradition an idol that marks our superiority and allows us to judge others? I know I am often tempted in this way myself. It's human *nature*, I think.

What about those homosexual acts?

So, what could we conclude about Paul's description of the unnatural sex in Romans 1:26-27?

1. It may not be his argument at all, but one that he is borrowing from Jewish philosophy to make his real point.
2. Even if it is his argument, he's saying that the same-gender sex he describes is:
   a. Rooted in man-crafted idol worship practices.
   b. An abandoning of heterosexual relations for homosexual (these people don't appear to be born gay) which could also be condemned as fornication or adultery.
   c. And these sexual worship practices then *lead* to a list of wickedness—note that they are separate this time from that list!

Conclusion

We've covered a lot of ground in this chapter, from Greek to

Jewish philosophy and including some more Scriptural readings. Let's try to summarize this pivotal passage.

1. The Stoic concept of Nature, likely familiar to Paul's audience, allows us to consider these verses in new ways. *"Unnatural intercourse"* may be defined as that which is opposed to an individual's disposition, breaks agreed-on social conventions, or is at odds with the created order.
2. Paul's *Epistle to the Romans* is about uniting the early church's Jews and Gentiles—first in moral equality before God, and then pointing them toward Jesus's fulfillment of the covenant and how this sets them free to live in *Love*, not under moral and cultural *Law*.
3. Finally, when we look carefully at the argument in the first chapter of Romans we may note two things:
    a. Paul appears to borrow from Jewish philosophical arguments in addition to Greek Stoicism, but maybe only in order to make a rhetorical negation of the entire premise
    b. However, if Paul does mean to use this argument to ban all same-sex relationships, then we should see them resulting in a life of wickedness and direct harm to others (ROMANS 1:29-30). Is this true of all our gay siblings in Christ today?

This passage is seen by many conservative Christians as the clearest prohibition of all homosexual relations (and the one that originally kept me on "side B"), yet I don't think it's as clearly condemning all homosexuality it looks on first read. After all this reading and research, the most I am comfortable saying is that Paul throws out references against same-sex acts, quite likely in an adulterous context, while he's building up an argument for the teachings that he really cares about.

Before we move on from our verse-by-verse study to a few broader observations in wrapping up, there's one more section of Romans I'd like to point out:

> Let us therefore no longer pass judgment on one another, but resolve instead never to put a stumbling block or hindrance in the way of another.
>
> I know and am persuaded in the Lord Jesus that nothing is unclean in itself; but it is unclean for anyone who thinks it unclean.
>
> — ROMANS 14:13-14

Here Paul returns to this concept of clean and unclean acts, but rather than uphold an external moral code he emphasizes the interior condition of the heart as most crucial. In context he's specifically discussing the eating of meat sacrificed to idols, which is one of only two commands passed on to the church by the Council of Jerusalem (ACTS 15).

In a similar pattern to many of the messages of Christ in the Gospels, the focus is not on the inherent quality of an external act, but on the orientation of our heart and our motives.

CHAPTER 9
The Spirit Speaking Through Experience

In some conservative circles the function of experience outside of Scripture in leading us to new insights is viewed with suspicion, and we are right to be cautious. After all, all of our experiences are subjective and individual, and we've seen some conclusions from experience turn out very poorly. However, the more I study Scripture, the more I see it as a collection of stories about how experiential encounters with God change both individuals and whole societies.

Before we conclude this discussion, I'd like to walk through a few examples of this as seen in the story of the early church as described in the book of Acts.

The Spirit leading in Acts

As I have continued reading the Bible, I have become convinced that the story of our faith is one of constant tension between the God who calls us to love and inclusion, and our human desire to fear and exclude.

From the beginning, we have always sought to claim God

for "us" against "them", only to be confronted by God breaking those boundaries. If we look carefully, we can see this happening throughout the story of Israel in the Tanakh and it becomes even clearer in the life and teachings of Jesus and his apostles. We then see this repeated over and over again in the centuries since Christ. It's not something we should feel guilty about, after all we're just part of the same story, but it is something to repent of—not to "feel sorry" about our actions, but to change our minds and move in a new direction.

In the book of Acts, as the community of Christ-followers begins to grow and develop their post-resurrection faith, we can see several examples of the Spirit leading people to include others against all prior understanding of their God and culture.

- Samaritans, and a practitioner of witchcraft (CH 8)
- The sexual minority, a eunuch, an Ethiopian (CH 8)
- The greatest persecutor and enemy of the church (CH 9)
- A paralytic Jew, traditionally seen as cursed by God (CH 9)
- A Roman centurion, both a foreigner and a member of the oppressing and occupying empire, one who had not converted to Judaism (CH 10)

Our stories here all start with a massive upheaval in the early faith community. Up until chapter 8 the young movement had been allowed to use the temple as an accepted sect of Judaism (it was a long time before they were seen as a separate religion). But the religious officials who had expected the teachings of Jesus to cease with his death became more and more opposed to the apostles' teachings. This culminated in the arrest and execution of Stephen, and the following persecution and scattering of the apostles which was led by a fanatical Pharisee named Saul.

Samaritans welcome the Gospel

As the church was forced out of Jerusalem, the Gospel began spreading to new areas. The first location described was Samaria, and the preacher was the Apostle Phillip.

Now, the Samaritans were more than just a neighboring tribe. To the Jews at the time they were sworn enemies and rival religionists, tracing their heritage back to the northern nation of Israel (sister nation to Judah). When the Assyrians began conquering the northern nation of Israel in 740 BCE, they deported many of the residents and brought in outsiders to mix with the original Israelites. The northern tribes also had their own unique Mosaic traditions and places of worship, and there was conflict over which group was most faithful to Yahweh. Samaritans, who are still around today, insist that they alone have the correct pre-captivity understanding of God. They also were the ones threatening the rebuilding of Jerusalem in the time of Nehemiah. At the time of the first century there were still occasional raids and violent conflicts back and forth between the cultural groups.

If Phillip went out from Israel to preach to Samaritans today, he would be entering the West Bank as governed by the Palestinian Authority. Here, where a pious Jew would be most unlikely to expect to find converts, we read:

> Philip went down to the city of Samaria and proclaimed the Messiah to them. The crowds with one accord listened eagerly to what was said by Philip, hearing and seeing the signs that he did, for unclean spirits, crying with loud shrieks, came out of many who were possessed; and many others who were

paralyzed or lame were cured. So there was great joy in that city.
— Acts 8:5-8

The first foreign-field missionary converts are the detested Samaritans, who are apparently more eager for the Gospel than the Jews in Jerusalem. What a surprise!

A practitioner of witchcraft switches allegiance

One of these new converts was a magician named Simon. Over time he had developed a following as "Simon the Great", and amazed many people with his skills. But under Philip's preaching, this man and his followers became believers. It took him a while to begin understanding that the Gospel power was not something for commercial purposes, but his devotion appeared to be sincere and he likely had to find new employment, a dramatic commitment to this new faith.

Here was a practitioner of witchcraft, condemned to death in the Tanakh (and consistently interpreted this way through much of church history—officially until 1951 in England), being named as one of the first foreign followers of Christ!

Inclusion of a sexual minority in the family of God

In Acts 8 we see the early church beginning to face persecution from a man named Saul, and the apostles are forced to move outward from Jerusalem. The apostle Phillip is directed by a message from an angel to set out on the road from Jerusalem to Gaza. There he encounters a man who is outside of the parameters of acceptance into God's people, according to Phillip's Judaic upbringing.

This man is a sexual minority, a eunuch, who is also an

Ethiopian. Males were commonly made into eunuchs for particular government roles to keep their loyalty undivided with a family. It's likely that this royal treasurer shared this story. He had come on a pilgrimage to Jerusalem, even though according to the Law he was prevented from being a part of worship due to his physical body as described in the Tanakh:

> "No one whose testicles are crushed or whose penis is cut off shall be admitted to the assembly of the Lord."
> — DEUTERONOMY 23:1

The blessings promised to a faithful Israel were described as the possession of land and the promise of descendants, consistent with ancient Near East cultural values. Yet being a eunuch meant that you had no descendants, and therefore no one to whom you could pass on your land. You were quite literally cut off from the blessing of God as promised to Abraham.

This very powerful individual, treasurer to the queen, made a pilgrimage in an upper class chariot all the way to Jerusalem, only to be excluded from worship. If we were to map out an on-foot route today using online tools, we'd be looking at 1,582 miles as the bird flies but 2,733 miles by land! That's likely a two-month long journey, riding in a dusty, noisy, bone-jarring chariot.

Note that we don't know exactly how this person is a eunuch, since Jesus referred to those who are born, made, and choose to be eunuchs as all under that label. But it's likely given the man's position that he has been made a eunuch surgically.

Phillip is compelled by the Spirit to approach the eunuch's chariot, and as he does so he hears him reading:

> like a lamb that is led to the slaughter,

> and like a *sheep that before its shearers* is silent,
>   so he did not open his mouth.
> By a *perversion of justice* he was taken away.
>   Who could have imagined his *future*?
> For he was *cut off* from the land of the living,
>   stricken for the transgression of my people.
>   — Isaiah 53:7-8 (NRSV)

Phillip asks him if he understands the passage, and the reply is "How could I, unless I have someone to guide me?" The eunuch urges Phillip to join him and explain what he is reading. He asks: *"About whom, may I ask you, does the prophet say this, about himself or about someone else?"* (Acts 8:34)

Why might this eunuch be so interested in this particular passage from the Prophets?

Maybe the language of *shearing* and being *cut off* would resonate with him. The passage speaks of one who has his *future* taken away. The ESV translates it as one with no *generation* to carry on his legacy as was so important at that time (and largely still today), in a perversion of justice. Maybe he would identify and relate to this imagery in a deep way, and wonder who the prophet could possibly be referring to in such validating language: *"Therefore I will allot him a portion with the great, and he shall divide the spoil with the strong;"* (Isaiah 53:12)

Phillip takes this cue to relay the gospel of Jesus. Here we see a man who was rejected by his people, stripped and humiliated, cut and wounded with scars that do not fade, one without physical descendants.

As they go along, the eunuch spots some water and asks:

"Look, here is water!

> What is to prevent me from being baptized?"
> — ACTS 8:36

Can you imagine that question being asked in a high, trembling, insecure voice? As from one who is desperate to be included, yet knows that tradition and Scripture are against him as both a foreigner and a eunuch? He had just returned from Jerusalem where he would have been denied entrance into worship. As an Ethiopian he would have been limited to the Courts of the Gentiles, yet as a eunuch even that would have been denied to him. After a two-month journey of devotion, he would have been forced to stare into the temple in longing, but feeling rejected by the God he was pursuing.

Author and pastor Brian McLaren, from whom I first heard this application, paraphrases the man's question:

> "I have just been rejected and humiliated in Jerusalem, but you have told me of a man who, like me, has no physical descendants, a scarred and wounded man who like me has been humiliated and rejected. Is there a place for me in his kingdom, even though I have an unchangeable condition that was condemned forever by the sacred Jewish Scriptures?"
> — BRIAN MCLAREN, "A NEW KIND OF CHRISTIANITY" p 183

Phillip's reaction in the text is breathtaking in its simplicity and audacity. As the horses are pulled to a stop in swirling dust and creaking of wood and leather, he answers not a word, but immediately leads the eunuch into the water to be baptized in equality before God.

They emerge dripping into a Spirit-filled new reality. Phillip is whisked away to the seashore by the Spirit of the Lord while the eunuch boards his chariot for home, rejoicing in this amazing and unexpected inclusion into the family of God.

> Do not let the foreigner joined to the Lord say,
> > "The Lord will surely separate me from his people";
> and do not let the *eunuch* say,
> > "I am just a dry tree."
> For thus says the Lord:
> "To the *eunuchs* who keep my sabbaths,
> > who choose the things that please me
> > and hold fast my covenant,
> I will give, in my house and within my walls,
> > a monument and a name
> > better than sons and daughters;
> I will give them an everlasting name
> > *that shall not be cut off."*
> > — Isaiah 56:3-5

A mystic vision for an analytical scholar

Remember, we're discussing the role of experience in our faith. Many conservatives are suspicious of any experiential elements in Christianity, preferring to focus only on the Bible. Yet that Bible is full of descriptions of how experiences with the Spirit change everything. In fact, you could say that our entire religion is founded on the idea that encounters with God should send us back to relearn what we always thought we knew. This story is one of the biggest examples.

I imagine most people reading this are roughly familiar with the Saul/Paul story. If you're not, read up—it's amazing! Let's take a quick look at the relevent bits here:

1. The first we hear of Saul, he's holding coats at Stephen's illegal, mob-driven, and brutal execution. The text says he approved of the killing.
2. He immediately becomes the biggest persecutor of the early church, leading the charge to arrest and jail the followers of this crazy new Judaic sect following what he saw as a dead and disgraced Jewish messiah-figure.
3. As the Apostles flee Jerusalem for what they hope will be safety elsewhere, Saul requests authority from the high priest to arrest followers of the Way in Syria.

Now here's where it gets interesting. Saul is approaching the end of his journey after two weeks on foot, with the city in sight.

Suddenly, "a light from heaven flashed around him!" He fell to the ground while a voice began speaking: "Saul, Saul, why do you persecute me?" He immediately recognizes this as a vision from God, but is confused because here he has been thinking that his mission has been one approved by God. He inquires as to the identity of this one he is persecuting, and is told that it is Jesus.

Can you imagine how world-shifting this would be for Saul? Here all of his scholarship and reliance on Scripture has led him to be certain of the rightness of his cause against the false teacher Jesus. Everything he has been taught since birth is about the One True God. Now he is faced with the revelation of Jesus co-existing with God. This, a man who he will later acknowledge is supposed to be especially cursed by God because of the form of his death (GALATIANS 3:13), was the very representation of God on earth!

Saul of course goes on to be renamed Paul and become the

church's most prominent missionary and the source of much of our New Testament. All through an encounter with the Spirit which forced him into a fourteen-year-long (GALATIANS 2:1) re-evaluation of his religious tradition and Scripture, re-reading everything in light of this new revelation.

Peter's dream changes the whole religion

During this time Peter has become the lead apostle in the church which is still distributed around the country after Saul's campaign had spread them out. He is living in Joppa on the coast.

Just a two-day journey up the coast lives a devout God-worshipping Roman Centurion. As a "God-fearer", he is not fully part of God's people as defined in Judaism, but he is held in high honor by the Jewish community. Once day this man, Cornelius, receives his own vision from an angel telling him to send for Peter to come and visit.

While Cornelius's men are still on the way, Peter goes up on the roof to pray. He is very hungry, and while waiting for his food he falls into a trance. He dreams of a large sheet being let down from heaven filled with all kinds of food which he is forbidden as a Jew to eat. He hears a voice which he recognizes as the Lord's, urging him to eat this food, and he refuses because he has "never eaten anything that is profane or unclean." He cannot get over his cultural and traditional upbringing to obey a direct command from God! The voice declares that "what God has made clean, you must not call profane."

When Peter wakes up, he is instructed by the Spirit to go with Cornelius's men when they arrive. Off he goes, to find that Cornelius has not only gathered his entire household around, but invited his relatives and close friends.

Now, to enter the house of even a righteous Gentile like this was to be made unclean as a Jew. However, Peter's new confidence from his dream makes him declare:

> "You yourselves know that it is unlawful for a Jew to associate with or to visit a Gentile; but God has shown me that I should not call anyone profane or unclean. So when I was sent for, I came without objection. Now may I ask why you sent for me?"
> — Acts 10:28-29

When he hears about Cornelius's vision, he begins to preach the gospel, starting with an amazing sentence for a follower of Judaism to utter:

> Then Peter began to speak to them: "I truly understand that God shows no partiality, but in every nation anyone who fears him and does what is right is acceptable to him."
> — Acts 10:34-35

What happens next is shocking even to Peter: as he is still speaking, "the Holy Spirit fell upon all who heard the word!" He insists on immediate baptism, declaring:

> "Can anyone withhold the water for baptizing these people who have received the Holy Spirit just as we have?"
> — Acts 10:47

It's hard for us Christians, two millennia removed from Peter's context, to fully grasp how big of a change this was. Gentiles, accepted by the Spirit and by an apostle without circumcision or other Jewish rites! This changed everything—as we see in Peter's fellow apostles initial reaction when they heard the news.

Peter called to account

This is all concluded in a meeting of the apostles where Peter is called to justify his non-Judaic behavior in baptizing non-Jews into the church. This may be the first heresy trial recorded in church history! It is certainly not a minor event. For his contemporaries, it seemed like Peter had just abandoned his faith and encouraged very ungodly behavior.

Peter did not go into theological arguments, nor did he pull up Scriptures to support his point. Instead, he told a personal story. By the description of his vision and then his experience of the Spirit coming upon the Gentiles before their baptism, they not only accept this account but begin rejoicing, saying *"Then God has given even to the Gentiles the repentance [turning/change] that leads to life."*

In fact, it was only in Antioch, where Gentiles were first included, that this little group of believers began to be called Christians (an insult originally, calling them *"little Christs"*). Now the story wasn't over at this point, as we see in Paul's letters his continual struggle to get the church to keep expanding their idea of who is in and out, and just how few rules they're expected to enforce. But the trajectory is clear: God is moving his people toward greater inclusion.

Conclusion

As we've seen, the Spirit led the members of the early church, those called themselves the Followers of the Way, far beyond their traditional understandings and interpretations of their Scriptures.

Professor and psychologist Richard Beck describes this section of Acts on his "Experimental Theology" blog as such:

> "It is almost as though the writer is answering a repeated question that might be framed as, "What about the So-and-So's? Do they get in?" And each time the answer is Yes. Samaritans? Yes. What about practitioners of Witchcraft? Yep. Those whose bodies are sexually non-normative? Yes, them too.
>
> And also, former Persecutors of the church. And finally, the crescendo to full inclusion of Gentiles, sealed by Peter's statements in 11:15-17 ("who was I to oppose God"?)."
>
> —RICHARD BECK (HTTP://BIT.LY/BECK-EUNUCHS)

This level of inclusion was very uncomfortable for the church. They struggled at various points with how to implement the Law and practices they still saw as valued in their Bibles, yet saw the Spirit leading in a new way.

In Paul's reflection on one of the pivotal meetings of a council, he insisted in very strong language ("You foolish Galatians! Who has bewitched you?") that God would have no extra restrictions placed on these believers. In the same epistle, the Letter to the Galatians, he went on to write:

> There is no longer Jew or Greek,
> > there is no longer slave or free,
> > > there is no longer male and female;
> > for all of you are one in Christ Jesus.
> > > —GALATIANS 3:1-2, 28

Here we have Paul confronting all of his societies divisions: race/religion, economic status and freedom, and gender distinctions. He declares that these boxes which were so important to culture at the time, and in our time as well, have no value before God because in Christ we are all one.

It is through experience that the Spirit can lead us today to see God in places that our tradition and our Scripture would have never led us to expect it. As Jesus said to his followers near the end of his time with them,

> "When the Spirit of truth comes,
> he will guide you into all the truth;
> for he will not speak on his own,
> but will speak whatever he hears,
> and he will declare to you the things that are to come."
> — JOHN 16:13

The question is, will we be willing to listen and prayerfully discern if the Spirit has something new to say to the church?

CHAPTER 10
Concluding Thoughts

We've now completed the look at the passages often cited in conservative Christian circles to exclude acceptance of gay Christians in the church and same-sex marriage in society. These are my answers to the specific questions I was asked, about how I can hold to the authority of Scripture while embracing my gay brothers and sisters in full fellowship.

I hope I have shown that the affirming position takes the Bible seriously, even if you remain firmly on the traditional side. Personally I don't believe that most of us humans change our minds based on logic and reason alone, but that it is in relationship and in listening to personal stories that our hearts can shift and grow. My prayer is that these expositions of Scripture may allow for more openness to that listening, and that we can all join together in spite of our different positions to support equal rights and condemnation of oppression and injustice wherever it is found.

While we have gone thoroughly through six passages of Scripture "against" homosexuality, I believe there are also passages which would directly support the acceptance of gay Christians in the church. I wanted to keep this book more focused, and with limited time and space I cannot cover those adequately at this time. However, I have added two appendixes to provide an overview of two general topics toward that end. I hope they are also useful for you in your journey.

Now, let's end with a brief summary of what has been covered in the book so far. Thank you so much for reading along with me, and I welcome your thoughts and dialogue any time.

What have we learned?

I can't speak for you, but in the process of this project I have learned and had reinforced a number of findings. I'll summarize here, and you can compare your experience to mine.

Can and should we re-examine the traditional interpretation?

We've seen that the Bible is a complex revelation that has never remained static in Christian community interpretation. There are many examples of previous ways of reading for social issues that we are grateful to have corrected (heliocentrism, slavery, antisemitism, interracial marriage, etc), and I suggest that this leaves open a possibility for re-examining our assumptions about the traditional condemnation of homosexuality.

We also know that there is much pain and division between gay people and the church. Regardless of where we may assign blame, this pain and conflict should drive us to make sure we are handling the situation as wisely and in as Christ-like a manner as possible.

Under the Law: The Tanakh

We examined three passages, taking into account some cultural context, Hebrew word study, and cross-referencing in the context of all of Scripture.

The Sin of Sodom and Gomorrah

The traditional reading of Genesis 19 has given us the word *sodomite* as describing certain male-with-male sexual acts. However, when we re-read carefully and look for references to the event throughout the Bible it seems clear to me that the focus of judgement is on communities who practice inhospitality, violence against the stranger, and neglecting care of the powerless and marginalized.

An Abomination in Leviticus 18

We explored the use of *abomination* throughout the Bible, and in the context that our key verse is found in. It seems reasonable to read this commandment as specifically excluding neighbor-nation idol worship practices involving male prostitutes for the set-apart nation of Israel.

The Death Penalty in Leviticus 20

Our second mention of "men lying with men" adds the death penalty as punishment. As disturbing as it is to consider some of the punishments in practice, by cross-referencing them we can add further evidence to connecting this command with a ban on male cult prostitutes.

Summarizing the Tanakh on homosexuality

I am convinced of the continued relevance of these passages as they speak against inhospitality, sexual abuse and violence, prostitution and sexual worship rituals. They don't seem to be related to the modern loving relationships I see modeled by my gay Christian friends in the church though.

Freedom in Christ: Does Paul condemn all same-gender sex?

Moving to the New Testament, we find three more passages that our contemporary translators have interpreted consistently against all expressions of homosexuality.

Male-bedders in 1 Timothy

Moving from Hebrew to Greek, we investigate this mysterious word *arsenokoites*. While the origin of the word leaves room for various interpretations, there is a good argument that in context we're reading a description of men who visit enslaved boy prostitutes. There are no gay Christians I know of who are advocating for this to be a legal part of society.

The Effeminate and Sodomites in 1 Corinthians

Taking the word *malakos* to mean soft in a metaphorical way, we see that some form of sexual behavior is most likely being condemned. However, when we see the popular evangelical NIV and ESV translations preferring to combine the terms as clearly meaning passive and active sexual partners, we may logically assume that it seems to be speaking about the abusive, temporal, and unequal relationship of pederasty, not a marriage context. We also see Paul advocating for the rule of Love rather than the rule of Law.

Unnatural Acts in Romans 1

Paul's main concern is unity in the church, and he knows that he must destroy the Jewish philosophy that "all sin comes from the idol worship (often including sexual worship practices) which they don't participate in so therefore they are more righteous by nature than the Gentiles." "No!" he says, and then shows them their equality in Christ's new covenant which leaves them no room to judge. Once again, Love trumps Law, both at the cross and in the church.

Summarizing the New Testament on homosexuality

Overall, it seems that Paul is more concerned about the early church finding the right balance between the freedom of Christ and abiding by a healthy moral code. He's trying to help this fledgling movement "write the Law on their hearts" instead of living by strict do's and don'ts.

Jesus overturned the convention of the Pharisees' *"religion of rules"* to establish a *"relationship of love"*, and to emphasize the Two Principles of Love to guide us instead of the 613 Commandments of the Law. This requires maturity, community, and maybe a bit of fumbling around from time to time to see how we may need to re-evaluate our traditions and assumptions to fit better with new realities. The early church was not alone in finding this difficult, and we need Paul's pastoral, counseling words today more than ever it seems.

Final thoughts

Regardless of your conclusions at the end of this study, I hope this project has helped you to see that affirming Christians, whether gay or allies, also take Scripture seriously. Let's keep this conversation going, while we remember that this may be an abstract debate for straight Christians but it can be a matter of life and death to our LGBT siblings in Christ.

In the words of our Apostle Paul, "the grace of the Lord Jesus be with you. My love be with all of you in Christ Jesus."

～ APPENDIX ～
Marriage in the Bible

Many conservative Christians are concerned about the redefinition of marriage as same-sex couples are included in the institution, and are calling for the upholding of the Biblical model of marriage. So what is marriage in the Bible, and what has it looked like in Christian societies throughout the centuries?

Here are the questions I want to ask in this section:

1. What is the model for marriage we are given in the Scriptures?
2. How has the church and surrounding society viewed marriage in the intervening centuries?
3. What seems to be the ultimate purpose of marriage?

Marriage as described in the Bible

The Bible is a vast library (the word literally comes from Latin, Greek and Phoenician for the plural of "book") of writings spanning many centuries and topics. There is not one text devoted to a complete and unchanging description of marriage, but there are many that give us insight at varying levels in into this social and spiritual institution.

Now, there are far too many relationships described in the Bible to go through all of them in this level of detail. We'll pick out some major sections and descriptions, along with some summaries and bullet points. Let's start at the beginning.

Looking at our two creation stories

There are two different creation accounts in the Bible. Even though I had read the Bible many times, I didn't recognize this until quite recently. There are different explanations Bible scholars propose for this, like one being a response to Mesopotamian myths and the other one later in response to Babylonian myths. It is important to recognize that they function both as independent narratives with their own focuses as well as parallel accounts that work together.

The first creation story: Genesis 1:1-2:4a

The first creation narrative in the Bible (GENESIS 1:1-2:4A) moves from the beginning with God alone to the grand finale with humankind. There is no reflection on a specific pair of humans, nor on marriage, but we can see that humans are the focus and end goal of the creative act.

> In the beginning when God began to create the heavens and the earth...
>
> — GENESIS 1:1 (NRSV VARIATION FROM TRANSLATION NOTES)

Some understand the phrase "the heavens and the earth" as a metaphorical description of "everything", as Shakespeare writes in Hamlet: "There are more things in heaven and earth...". We may think of it as a spectrum, with everything on every plane of our world, every string-theory dimension of reality, and both physical and spiritual understandings originating with God, the *"alpha and omega"* (again an inclusive spectrum concept). Some call this a *"merism"*, a figure of speech used in law, rhetoric, biology, and Biblical poetry:

> In rhetoric a *merism* is the combination of two contrasting words, to refer to an entirety. For example, when we mean to say that someone searched thoroughly, everywhere, we often say that someone searched high and low...
>
> Merisms are conspicuous features of Biblical poetry. For example, in Genesis 1:1, when God creates "the heavens and the earth" (KJV), the two parts combine to indicate that God created the whole universe. Similarly, in Psalm 139, the psalmist declares that God knows "my downsitting and mine uprising", indicating that God knows all the psalmist's actions.
> — https://en.wikipedia.org/wiki/Merism

This grand, majestic and poetic account cumulates in the making of humankind in the image of God:

> Then God said,
> > "Let us make humankind in our image,
> > > according to our likeness..."
>
> So God created humankind in his image,
> > in the image of God he created them;
> > > male and female he created them.
>
> — Genesis 1:26a, 27

What do we know from this creation account? We know that all humans are made in the image of God, not God made in the image of humans. That all humanity is created in the likeness of God the one-and-three ("our"). That all humanity, the spectrum included in "male and female", is created in equality without hierarchy and declared good:

> God saw everything that he had made,
>> and indeed, it was very good.
>
> — GENESIS 1:31A

In creation *everything* is called good by the Creator. No matter what happens as the story of Scripture continues, that declaration of goodness remains God's opinion about his creation.

Why could it be helpful to recognize a spectrum rather than a binary designation in the phrase *"male and female"*? Consider those who are born as Intersex (the "I" in the more complete acronym LGBTQIA) with inconclusive genitalia. Or some Transgender folks who have the physical genitalia of one gender, and the chromosomes and brain-structure of another. If we are all created in the image of God, and declared good, then maybe *"male and female"* is a non-dualistic container, a *merism*, of the variety of the good creation even while we recognize that the majority of people fit comfortably near each of the traditional ends of the spectrum.

Finally, note that the entirety of the first self-contained creation account is about "humankind" in general, with no mention of a named pair of individuals nor a description of marriage. Now let's move on the second creation story, starting immediately after the first passage, to see what is shared and what is unique about its narrative and focus.

The second creation story: Genesis 2:4b-2:24

> Then the Lord God formed *the adam* [human] from the dust of *the adamah* [ground/humus], and breathed into the nostrils the breath of life; and *the adam* became a living being.
>
> Then the Lord God said,
> "It is not good that *the adam* should be alone;
> I will make a helper—a corresponding partner."
>
> — GENESIS 2:7, 18 (AUTHOR'S MORE LITERAL PARAPHRASE)

In the second creation narrative starting at Genesis 2:5, at first only one human is created: the *adam* (generic word for *human*, not used as a proper name until verse 20) from *adamah* (Hebrew for *ground* or *humus*). Then the Lord God remarks that it is not good for the human to *be alone*. There is no mention of the need for procreation, but rather of companionship and relationship. This is a love story, not a pragmatic way to fill up the world with children—remember, the command to "be fruitful and multiply" is part of the self-contained first creation story and does not seem to apply to this second story's main point.

A corresponding companion is sought for the currently ungendered human among the animals. When this is not found, a suitable partner is made by drawing another human out of the first. While there is a very good argument from cross-referencing other verses that the traditional word "rib" is likely better translated "side", regardless of the exact term it's important to note how the origin was from a place of equality.

The KJV's original translation decision of "helpmeet" has been often misunderstood to imply "assistant/lower partner" instead of "appropriate partner." But if we cross-reference the text, we find that this Hebrew phrase is used for one who comes in support of another—often the stronger coming to the aid of the weaker, as in describing God or an army coming to reinforce someone in battle. Equality, equivalency and relationship are the primary emphases in this account.

> "This at last is bone of my bones
> and flesh of my flesh;
> this one shall be called *ishshah* [woman],
> for out of *ish* [man] this one was taken."
> — GENESIS 2:23

The passage concludes with the man and woman coming back together to make one flesh. The particular is subsumed in union.

In neither creation narrative is a marriage ceremony mentioned, nor are any other models of relationship described in negative or positive terms. To use these stories as prescriptive for every relationship seems to take the meaning beyond what is written. Since procreation was important to cultures at the time, and marriage understood in the context of inheritance and multiplying, heterosexual relationships seem to be the assumed model. If anything, it seems to me that there is a de-emphasis on the importance of being either male or female, and a focus on our shared humanity and need for relationship.

Marriage amongst the patriarchs

Before the Law was given at Mount Sinai, forming what we now recognize as Judaism, we have several very important figures in Jewish and Christian history: Abraham, Isaac and Jacob. Their marriages share little with the Christian ideal today.

Abram and Sarai and Hagar

Abram (later better known as Abraham) apparently married his half-sister Sarai (later Sarah), the daughter of his own father, as he describes to Abimelech in Genesis 20:12. This form of coupling is explicitly forbidden as cursed in Deuteronomy 27:22, yet the relationship between Abraham and Sarah is never condemned and can be seen as one of the best pictures of marriage in the Tanakh.

Later we see Sarai give her servant to Abram to produce a son for them, as she was barren. While we see family and ancestral conflict arise later from this decision, the typical ancient near-east practice itself is not clearly condemned in the Bible. The only aspect that is taken negatively is the lack of faith that action implies, not the method of conception itself.

After Sarah dies, Abraham takes another wife, Keturah, with whom he has six sons (and unspecified daughters perhaps?). In the description of his distribution of inheritance, the "sons of his concubines", apparently specified in addition to the sons of his wives, are given gifts (GENESIS 25:1-6).

Isaac and Rebecca

We hear very little about Isaac compared to his more famous father and son. Our narrative in the middle of Genesis paints a very different picture of one who did not seem to have the same procreative drive as the typical patriarch. He appears to have no interest in marriage, as his father has to take the initiative to find him a suitable dynasty partner at age 40. They have one birth, of twins, and no further children are recorded whether from this marriage or from the concubines or other servants which were typically impregnated by the head of the household at the time.

Jacob and Leah and Rachel and Bilhah and Zilpah

Jacob gets the procreation narrative back on track with two official wives and two official concubines. All four women contribute to producing the twelve male legal heirs which lead to the twelve tribes of Israel. Again, while there is plenty of family rivalry to give us a dim view of the benefits of this arrangement, there is no suggestion anywhere in the story that God has anything against the multiple married and unmarried partners in the story. The great blessing promised to Abraham, of his descendants uncountable as stars in the heavens, appears to be on track because of, not in spite of, this depiction of marriage structure.

Judah and Tamar

We will look at the story of Judah and Tamar in more detail in a later chapter on Leviticus 20:13. In brief, Judah is obligated to impregnate his daughter-in-law after his sons die without giving her a son. Though he ends up doing this through her trickery, he honors her persistence in seeking justice once it's all revealed. This sexual relationship which seems so foreign and immoral to our modern ears is never condemned in Scripture. In fact, Tamar shows up as one of the few women honored as ancestors of Jesus in the gospel of Matthew, along with Rahab the prostitute.

Onan and Tamar

Judah was Tamar's third option to have a child, after her husband dies and she is initially given to her brother-in-law:

> Then Judah said to Onan, "Go in to your brother's wife and perform the duty of a brother-in-law to her; raise up offspring

for your brother." But since Onan knew that the offspring would not be his, he spilled his semen on the ground whenever he went in to his brother's wife, so that he would not give offspring to his brother. What he did was displeasing in the sight of the Lord, and he put him to death also.
— GENESIS 38:8-10

Tamar had married Judah's firstborn son Er, but he died and she became a widow. According to Levirate marriage rules, she was then given to Judah's next son, Onan, so that he would produce a son through Tamar to carry on Er's line. Onan's sacred duty was to provide the offspring in the name of his brother.

But Onan wanted nothing to do with producing and providing for a child that would not be known as his. He made sure Tamar would not be impregnated during sex using a basic form of birth control, as described above. This rejection of his duty, and the wasting of his *seed* ("zera") on the ground, was considered so despicable that we see his fate described as ending in death, attributed directly to this act.

Throughout most of history (until the 1600's), it was assumed that men carried the entire "seed" of children, and that the woman merely incubated the child until born. Therefore, the spilling of the seed on the ground was seen as a form of abortion. You can imagine the cultural view on any kind of non-procreational sexual relationships. It was far more important to prioritize child-bearing when populations were low and death-rates from disease, war, poverty, etc, were high. Some Christian groups today believe these prohibitions against all forms of birth control continue to apply (by Roman Catholic official doctrine and "Quiverful" Protestants, for example), but most Christians act in practice at least as if this was a cultural/contextual situation and not a binding principal for all time.

Marriage described in the Law

Old Testament accounts and ordinances given in the Law assume very different understandings of marriage and procreation than we're used to today. Here are a few examples of practices regulated by the Law:

- If a man decides he does not like his new wife, and accuses her of not being a virgin, a trial is held. If she can prove her innocence, he pays money to her family. If she cannot, she is stoned to death. DEUTERONOMY 22:13-20
- A rapist who assaults an unengaged woman is required to pay her family for her and get married. The woman has no say in the matter. DEUTERONOMY 22:28-29
- If a man's brother dies with no heir from his wife, he must marry his sister-in-law and provide a son for his brother's line (known as Levirate marriage). DEUTERONOMY 25:5-10

Now, if we take the cultural context into account, and compare with other ancient practices and societies, these laws are often an improvement over earlier and neighboring cultures. We can still learn a lot from even these parts of the Law which we would never consider following today. However, it is very difficult to support our modern ideas of marriage by looking at Mosaic Law. Bear in mind that Deuteronomy repeatedly declares all these statutes and ordinances to be required by the Lord for blessing. They are found in amongst commands to love God, avoid worshiping idols, and kill off other tribes.

Marriages of the kings

In 2 Samuel 12:8 the prophet Nathan says that God gave Saul's wives to David, and would give him more if he asked. Solomon's multitude of wives and concubines seem to be a problem for idol-worship and political treaty reasons, not anything inherently wrong with the quantity.

The marriage most focused on the relationship between a single man and a single woman among the kings of Israel and Judah is the partnership of Ahab and Jezebel, not the best model of a Godly couple. It's hard to make a case from these examples that polygamy on its own was considered to be a problem during this period of God's chosen people.

Marriage according to Jesus

Once again, it's difficult to see Jesus affirming the 1950s American ideal of the nuclear family. His ministry was about expanding our idea of what it meant to live in relationship and community, often calling out traditional arrangements as a barrier to discipleship.

Jesus on family

In the narratives of Jesus we find recorded in our four gospels, there is little celebration of the traditional family, and some apparent criticism of family obligations and constraints.

When Jesus is interrupted in his sermons by his mother and brothers, apparently with the intent to restrain him as an insane person, he rejects their claim of authority and relationship by replacing them with his disciples as his "family", saying that "whoever does the will of my Father in heaven is my brother and sister and mother" (MARK 3:31-35). This is in direct opposition to the commandment in the Law to "honor your father and your mother" (EXODUS 20:12), and he risks the harsh consequences of stoning to death for familiar rebellion (DEUTERONOMY 21:18-21). He clearly understood that his obligation to God's rule superseded his family's claim, and he modeled this for his followers.

Jesus clearly understood how radical and disruptive his teachings were to normal societal structures and expectations. He recognized the dramatic impact his words would have, that in following Christ his disciples would often have to give up their old relationships, their families of origin would reject them, and that their new "families" would be formed out of those who also followed Jesus, even including members they would formerly have considered enemies:

> "Do not think that I have come to bring peace to the earth;
> I have not come to bring peace, but a sword.
>
> *"For I have come to set a man against his father,*
> *and a daughter against her mother,*
> *and a daughter-in-law against her mother-in-law;*
> *and one's foes will be members of one's own household.*
>
> "Whoever loves father or mother more than me is not worthy of me; and whoever loves son or daughter more than me is not worthy of me;"
> — MATTHEW 10:34-37

The parallel passage in Luke is even stronger: "Whoever comes to me and does not *hate* father and mother, wife and children, brothers and sisters, yes, and even life itself, cannot be my disciple" (LUKE 14:26). Most LGBT Christians, and many of their straight allies, have experienced the pain of these truths in their own lives as they have followed Christ in ways which have brought rejection from their families and faith communities.

There are many other examples in the gospels where Jesus emphasized the new "family values" in the kingdom, warning his disciples that their cultural expectations of duty and love to their family members should no longer come first. They were to abandon their traditional family obligations (burying and even saying goodbye to family members—LUKE 9:57-62) and pledge full allegiance to their new "family" made up of those who also followed Christ.

Jesus's focus on the family in the kingdom of God is one that questions the traditions and assumptions of both his time and ours, dramatically redefining it in very uncomfortable ways.

Jesus on divorce and remarriage

One of the passages commonly used to affirm heterosexual marriage is Jesus' teaching on divorce in reaction to a testing question by some religious scholars:

> Some Pharisees came, and to test him they asked, "Is it lawful for a man to divorce his wife?"
>
> He answered them, "What did Moses command you?"
>
> They said, "Moses allowed a man to write a certificate of dismissal and to divorce her."
>
> But Jesus said to them, "Because of your hardness of heart he wrote this commandment for you. But from the beginning of creation, 'God made them male and female.' 'For this reason a man shall leave his father and mother and be joined to his wife, and the two shall become one flesh.' So they are no longer two,

> but one flesh. Therefore what God has joined together, let no one separate."
>
> Then in the house the disciples asked him again about this matter. He said to them, "Whoever divorces his wife and marries another commits adultery against her; and if she divorces her husband and marries another, she commits adultery."

— MARK 10:2-12

First, it's important to remember that this question and answer session is not about marriage, but about divorce. In context it does not appear to be meant to define the specific make-up of a relationship, but only speak to the reason for the uniting together of two individuals, and the ideal intention for lasting commitment. As we discussed in the earlier coverage of Genesis 2, *"for this reason"* seems to refer to the human need for companionship, not procreation or social expectation. If this passage was meant to define marriage as only valid between one man and one woman, I would expect to see teachings against polygamy as well, which is never condemned in Scripture.

As for divorce, Jesus is definitively rejecting the clearly laid out Law of Moses in favor of a more general divine principle. In defiance of accepted rhetoric and interpretive conventions, he uses a verse which doesn't directly mention either marriage or divorce to override ones which do. This is an interesting precedence he sets for furture interpretions by his disciples through the centuries.

Once again, let's take the context of Jesus's words into account. In first century Judaism there were different interpretations of the Law regarding divorce. New Testament professor Dr. Gary Burge of Wheaton College points out three teachings by Rabbis of the time:

1. Rabbi Shammai said only adultery justified divorce.
2. Rabbi Hillel allowed that *"a man may divorce his wife even if she burned his soup… or spoiled a dish for him."*
3. Rabbi Akiba accepted divorce *"if he should find a woman fairer than his wife."*[34]

As was common with the questions asked by Pharisees and Sadducees in the gospels, Jesus was being asked which interpretive camp he belonged to. In the Mark passage he takes Rabbi Shammai's teaching and runs with it even farther, allowing no valid reasons for divorce, even adultery.

There are four statements on divorce in the New Testament, three in the synoptic gospels and one from Paul. If we are careful to look at each one in its own context and analyze their logic directly, we may find some variation which makes our understanding of the teachings on divorce less certain:

1. In the Mark passage—the first gospel written and likely a reference text for the other two synoptic accounts—divorce is given no justification, and remarriage is equivalent with adultery.
2. Matthew takes this same statement, but softens it back to agree with Rabbi Shammai by allowing for divorce and remarriage in the case of adultery in the original marriage (MATTHEW 19:9).

---

34 *"Directions: You're Divorced—Can You Remarry?"*, Gary M. Burge, Christianity Today, October 1999

3. Luke omits the story about the testing and quotation of Genesis, and simply prohibits remarriage without directly condemning divorce (LUKE 16:18).
4. Finally, Paul seems to directly override Jesus's instructions ("I and not the Lord") to instruct the Corinthians that divorce and remarriage is allowed between believers and unbelievers (1 CORINTHIANS 7:1-16).

As Jesus's own disciples point out, the strictest of these teachings may act like a deterrent against marriage entirely. It's interesting that there has never been a major church denomination which has fully excluded any possibility of divorce in all circumstances. We might speculatate that either this passage is hyperbole in the vein of "cut off your own hand if it causes you to sin", or that Jesus had a dim view of marriage in his culture.

Jesus and Paul on celibacy and "eunuchs"

Instead, Jesus appears to prefer his followers to remain unmarried, and many of his subsequent followers agreed. Paul certainly made it clear that celibacy was his preference for the church.

In one significant passage recorded only in Matthew, Jesus answers the concern of the disciples about the unreasonableness of marriage without divorce by talking about counter-cultural concept of eunuchs:

> His disciples said to him, "If such is the case of a man with his wife, it is better not to marry."

> But he said to them, "Not everyone can accept this teaching, but only those to whom it is given. For there are eunuchs who have been so from birth, and there are eunuchs who have

been made eunuchs by others, and there are eunuchs who have made themselves eunuchs for the sake of the kingdom of heaven. Let anyone accept this who can."

— MATTHEW 19:10-12

Jesus speaks of three kinds of "eunuchs"—men who did not marry women in the first century. Castrated men were often trusted in government positions at the time because they did not have divided loyalty with a family (we cover this further in the next chapter). Men who give up marriage for "the sake of the kingdom" are honored, in a way which seems to imply it was Jesus's preference for his followers. But there is a third kind of eununch mentioned, those "who have been so from birth".

There are two explanations we could consider for what this description is meant to define.

First, according to Jewish tradition as passed down in the Talmud and Mishna, there is a description of a *"seris hamah"* ("sun eunuch", one who was a eunuch from the first time he appeared in the sun, a congenital eunuch). According to a recent analysis of ancient descriptions, the term is likely describing some forms of congenital intersex conditions wherein some kind of genetic or hormonal abnormality results in a child which does not develop sexually in a typical way.

Second, some scholars have found both Greek and Christian commentary from the first few centuries CE which appear to describe "natural eunuchs" (noncastrated) who are physically capable of procreation but have no interest in women. These men also could be employed to guard royal harems since they would have proven no interest in interfering with the king's exclusive right to the women. While speculative, it's possible that Jesus could even be referring to men who were born gay.

Regardless of the answer to this question, it is clear that Jesus is both affirming the value of remaining unmarried and both recognizing and valuing sexual minorities in his culture which would have been unusual for many rabbis of the time even if the men were not gay.

Marriage in Acts

The only two Christ-following couples we find described in the book of Acts—the recording of the early church life and practice—do not fit neatly into our modern concept of the ideal nuclear family.

The first pair is Ananias and Sapphira. In the early days of the church, the "whole group of believers" (ACTS 4:32) are sharing their possessions in common, making sure that no one lacks for anything while others have resources to help. Yet this one couple is described as deciding to hold back some of their resources to provide for their own family, while claiming that they are contributing to the same level as others. This prioritization of the nuclear family above the greater community is strongly condemned and leads to the death of the couple.

The second pair are Aquila and Priscilla, Paul's friends in Corinth. They also do not fit into the either the 1st century or modern conservative Christian formulas, being described as a migratory professional childless couple hosting a male bachelor instead of the typical multi-generational household of the time.

Marriage in the Epistles

Paul and the other writers of the epistles have much more to say on the subject of marriage than the gospels. It's certainly a mixed bag, with a lot of idealization of celibacy and mixed messages on the roles of the partners in marriage.

The only mention in Scripture against polygamy are found in the letters of 1 Timothy and Titus, where bishops (overseers over local pastors) and deacons are recommended to have one wife. It's unclear whether this has anything to do with divorce and remarriage, or if it's only recommending against multiple wives at one time. Personally, I think polygamy treats women unequally, has great potential for abuse, and has much less positive to be said for it than same-sex marriage. But a ban on polygamy for all Christians cannot be found in a strict reading of the Bible.

There are instructions for equal rights within marriage, and there are instructions which place a wife under the authority of a husband. The co-existance of these directives in different epistles are both why some scholars think the epistles cover a wider range of time and teachings than conservative estimates, and why we have both complementarian and equalitarian camps citing Scripture as their authority.

Even in these more prescriptive books, precise forms of marriage do not appear as clearly described as we might like.

Marriage in Christian history since the 1st century

Since the completion of the canon of Scripture as we see it today, we also have volumes of teachings and interpretations of the Bible passed down through the centuries. It can be helpful to see how the Body of Christ has understood the Scriptural witness on the subject of marriage over time. While this topic could (and does) fill multiple volumes on its own, I'd like to touch on just a few periods which show how differently we have understood Scripture on marriage over the centuries.

Early church fathers

The attitude of theologians, bishops and pastors in the first few centuries of the church on the subject of marriage is in dramatic contrast to some of our modern positions.

Celibacy and abstinance from sex was considered the ideal for all Christians. It was even considered a heresy at one point to accept that marriage had equal value to celibacy.

Around the 4th century there were prohibitions on marriage once you were ordained in the the church. Some councils, for example the Spanish Council of Elvira (c. 305), forbid all bishops, priests and deacons to have sex or beget children with their wives on pain of losing their ordination.

While there were varying teachings, and the practice of them was also very loose at times, there was a consistent message from very early in the church that marriage was considered less holy than celibacy.

Marriage and sexuality in the medieval church

While there may be a perception that the Roman Catholic Church has always held marriage to be a sacrament and that ordained leaders must be celibate, this is not true.

The Western Church had no prohibitions against polygamy amongst clergy until the 8th century. It wasn't until 1123 that priests were forbidden to have concubines and wives, and only in 1563 was marriage finally prohibited for all clergy in the Roman Catholic Church.

Marriages in the time of Christ and for much of human

history were considered primarily to be economic contracts. During the collapse of the Roman empire in the 5th century the church took over marriage and redefined it as a holy union. It was declared as one of the seven sacraments of the Catholic Church in 1215, but it was not until 1547 that it was decreed to be performed in public by a priest before witnesses.

We can also find some scholarship which has pointed out evidence that attitudes toward gay couples were not uniformly negative in the church until the 13th century, around the time of the Inquisition. Until this point there seem to be some periods when same-sex relationships even amongst clergy were accepted or even celebrated. There are church liturgies for "spiritual brotherhoods" from the 12th century which looked remarkably like other marriages. There is still much scholarly debate about the practice of these same-sex unions though.

Marriage among the Reformers

As the Protestant Reformers reacted against some of the abuses and theological problems of their contemporary Church, one area they redefined was marriage. Beyond deciding that clergy could marry, and entering into this state himself, Martin Luther also rejected the idea of marriage as a sacrament of the church. He insisted that "marriage is a civic matter. It is really not, together with all its circumstances, the business of the church. It is so only when a matter of conscience is involved." He taught that a marriage was based on the mutual consent of a man and woman, and that a couple which cohabited were automatically to be considered married.

John Calvin viewed government magistrates as ministers of God equal with clergy, and was very interested in the details of marriage law as a lawyer himself. He also saw marriage as a contract more associated with government than with the church. He emphasized mutal attraction in marriage and the removal of it as a sacrament as well.

Many variations on marriage emerged during the splitting of the Church into various Protestant groups, and teachings from Scripture became much more varied in interpretation.

Marriage in the 20th century American church

It was only in the 17th and 18th centuries that Enlightenment thinkers talking about marrying for love rather than wealth or status. It became one of the cornerstones of the modern "right to pursue happiness".

Once the middle class began to grow, and our interest in innate human rights and privileges developed, our understandings and rules around marriage began changing rapidly. We now generally encourage divorce in abusive situations, women have equal rights before the law in marriage and divorce proceedings, just since 1970, and birth control has shifted our practice and understanding of marriage dramatically too.

Historians say that much of what the conservative Christian church pictures as the unchanging ideal for marriage comes out of a rose-tinted view of white suburban 1950s American with little understanding of just how novel that image is. For centuries marriage has looked more like economic contracts, polygamy, multi-generational households, and often seen by the church as less ideal than being single.

We should be careful in the church today to not put marriage on too high of a pedestal. It is a gift, but it can also be a barrier for many of our fellow believers to full fellowship in a church.

Even the conservative traditionalist pastor and author Kevin DeYoung, writing his argument against same-sex marriage, decries the modern "idolatry of the nuclear family":

> But, of course, none of this can be possible without uprooting the idolatry of the nuclear family, which holds sway in many conservative churches. The trajectory of the New Testament is to relativize the importance of marriage and biological kinship. A spouse and a minivan full of kids on the way to Disney World is a sweet gift and a terrible god. If everything in Christian community revolves around being married with children, we should not be surprised when singleness sounds like a death sentence.
> — Kevin DeYoung, *"What Does the Bible Really Teach about Homosexuality?"* (p. 119)

What is the purpose of marriage?

There are various arguments made in different Christian traditions about the purpose of marriage.

Some say marriage is for the purpose of procreation, and therefore any marriage which is not capable of generating children is not valid. However, this is both inconsistent with Genesis 2's emphasis on companionship and it doesn't take into account marriages which are barren or when partners marry late in life. It also makes a relationship about functionality rather than about love. This view of marriage was often used against barren women in Jesus's time, justifying divorce if there were no children.

Others seem to emphasize sex, whether it's explicitly stated or not. Growing up in the conservative church, there was a lot of focus on waiting for sex until you were married and hardly anything about other aspects of the marriage relationship. In conversations about same-sex marriage with conservative friends I've also noticed a focus on sex and lust. However, when I listen to my LGBT friends they have a broader understanding of the purpose of marriage. They do not focus on the satisfying of lust (marriage is not needed for that!), but rather on a desire for deep lifelong commitment, self-sacrificing love, and a recognition of the sacredness of the bond before their friends and the world.

When Jesus was confronted by those who saw the covenent of Israel to be about following rules rather than the gift of a good relationship with God, he sought to redefine their understanding of what the Law was for:

> Then he said to them,
> > "The sabbath was made for humankind,
> > and not humankind for the sabbath"
>
> — MARK 2:27

Just as Jesus asked about the purpose of the Sabbath, we may ask whether humans were made to fit into an absolute, unchanging institution called marriage, or whether marriage was created to help humans—perhaps including gay humans?—live wisely and well in this world.

I think the exact form of marriage we have been used to, emphasizing an independent nuclear family isolated from other family members, is a social construct from the 1950s. It's not a bad thing, but it's not a universal standard either if you research history. It used to be more focused on property rights and passing down lines than on love and chosen commitment.

For me, marriage is about covenanted commitment before God between two people, to care for and encourage the life and love of the other, in self-sacrificing love, which reflects the love of God for each one of us. I believe there need be no difference there for same-sex couples, if we can see it outside of our contemporary cultural biases.

Why same-sex *marriage* though?

It's a good question—if we're going to accept same-gender couples in our society, do we have "change marriage" to allow them there too? Can't we just have civil unions or a different name?

Very briefly, here are a few things to consider:

- Marriage in general is being seen as less relevant or sacred by much of our society today, and certainly treated that way in practice by much of our church itself when we look at divorce rates. Shouldn't we welcome those who are eager to enter into the institution?
- Same-sex marriage gives our gay Christian friends good role models of how to be gay, follow Christ, and have a healthy family relationship too. Giving it an equal footing removes the support for forcing gay people to enter straight marriages as their own option for marriage, which they have .
- It's a sign of equality before God, as humans. Limiting it to "heterosexual couples only" implicitly denies equality. A policy of "separate but equal" is not something we want to return to, as it supported much abuse under Jim

Crow laws.
- Access to marriage gives equal access to legal, political, and family rights. For those worried about adoption or foster care, studies have shown that two parents of any gender are better than one, and that we have great need of stable families to care for children in this country.

As we've looked at in this chapter, we've already seen many changes in the institution of marriage in recorded history. This latest redefinition is simply one in a long line of changes in this human institution, and does not have to be seen as an "attack":

- Multiple wives and substitute servant partners were considered normal and expected in the Tanakh.
- Levirate marriage, mandated by the Law, expected a man to marry his sister-in-law when his brother died, and have more children for him.
- Divorces were granted for any reason from the man in Jesus' time, and often because there were no children. Jesus had a big problem with this functional view of marriage. We may also assume that the Samaritan woman at the well (John 4) had been rejected over and over because of infertility, and Jesus offered her life and acceptance with no condemnation even though he knew that she would be perceived with no value by others who knew.
- Marriages have been seen as primarily economic and political transactions in many cultures through the centuries.
- Arranged marriages have been the norm for most people in the world.
- American slaves were encouraged to marry by their

Christian owners, but their marriages were not given legal status and the relationships and children were often ignored when buying and selling.
- Mixed-race marriages were strictly forbidden in most states in the US until 1948, and it wasn't until 1967 that the Supreme Court overturned the remaining 16 state laws that forbid intermarriage of all races. Appeals for permission to reinstate the bans continued until Alabama gave up in 2000 (note that Alabama is now back in the news arguing against same-sex marriage). Arguments from tradition and the Bible were often central in arguments against interracial marriage, exemplified by conservative Bob Jones University's policies.

More discussion of how welcoming same-gender marriage can at the same time improve the institution for all of us can be found in Bishop Gene Robinson's book "God Believes in Love".

Conclusion

As we've seen in this chapter, "Biblical marriage" does not look very much like what we're used to in conservative Christian ideals, and the institution itself has changed repeatedly over time. Maybe we can relax about prior definitions, and look to see how we can help our fellow Christians, and ourselves, to continue moving our focus toward providing life-giving and loving environment rather than following a set of rigid rules.